Anthropology Research and Developments

Repatriation of Indian Human Remains

Efforts of the Smithsonian Institution

Anthropology Research and Developments

Additional books in this series can be found on Nova's website under the Series tab.

Additional E-books in this series can be found on Nova's website under the E-book tab.

ANTHROPOLOGY RESEARCH AND DEVELOPMENTS

REPATRIATION OF INDIAN HUMAN REMAINS

EFFORTS OF THE SMITHSONIAN INSTITUTION

LAURENT B. DAVILLE

EDITOR

NOVINKA

New York

For permission to use material from this book please contact us:
Telephone 631-231-7269; Fax 631-231-8175
Web Site: http://www.novapublishers.com

Additional color graphics may be available in the e-book version of this book.

LIBRARY OF CONGRESS CATALOGING-IN-PUBLICATION DATA

ISBN: 978-1-62618-258-5

Published by Nova Science Publishers, Inc. † New York

CONTENTS

PREFACE

The Smithsonian Institution holds a large number of Indian human remains and culturally significant objects as part of its museum collections. These human remains and objects have long been a concern for many Indian tribes and Native Hawaiian communities, who have been determined to provide an appropriate resting place for their ancestors. In 1989, the National Museum of the American Indian Act (NMAI Act) was enacted, in part to address these concerns. This book is a study of the Smithsonian Institution's efforts to repatriate Indian human remains, with a focus on ways to expedite the process and recommendations from the Government Accountability Office (GAO). The GAO reviewed museum records, including 171 repatriation case reports, and interviewed the Smithsonian, the Repatriation Review Committee, and tribal officials.

Chapter 1 – The National Museum of the American Indian Act of 1989 (NMAI Act), as amended in 1996, generally requires the Smithsonian Institution to inventory and identify the origins of its Indian human remains and objects placed with them (funerary objects) and repatriate them to culturally affiliated Indian tribes upon request. It also creates a special committee to oversee this process. According to the Smithsonian, two of its museums—the American Indian and the Natural History Museums— have items that are subject to the act. GAO was asked to determine (1) the extent to which the Smithsonian has fulfilled its repatriation requirements, (2) how the special committee provisions have been implemented, and (3) the number of human remains and objects that have been repatriated and reasons for any that have not. GAO reviewed museum records, including 171 repatriation case reports, and interviewed Smithsonian, Repatriation Review Committee, and tribal officials.

Chapter 2 – Statement of Anu K. Mittal, Director, Natural Resources an Environment, Government Accountability Office.

Chapter 3 – Testimony of Kevin Gover, Director, National Museum of the American Indian.

In: Repatriation of Indian Human Remains ISBN: 978-1-62618-258-5
Editor: Laurent B. Daville

Chapter 1

SMITHSONIAN INSTITUTION: MUCH WORK STILL NEEDED TO IDENTIFY AND REPATRIATE INDIAN HUMAN REMAINS AND OBJECTS*

United States Government Accountability Office

WHY GAO DID THIS STUDY

The National Museum of the American Indian Act of 1989 (NMAI Act), as amended in 1996, generally requires the Smithsonian Institution to inventory and identify the origins of its Indian human remains and objects placed with them (funerary objects) and repatriate them to culturally affiliated Indian tribes upon request. It also creates a special committee to oversee this process. According to the Smithsonian, two of its museums—the American Indian and the Natural History Museums— have items that are subject to the act. GAO was asked to determine (1) the extent to which the Smithsonian has fulfilled its repatriation requirements, (2) how the special committee provisions have been implemented, and (3) the number of human remains and objects that have been repatriated and reasons for any that have not. GAO

* This is an edited, reformatted and augmented version of United States Government Accountability Office, Publication No. GAO-11-515, dated May 2011.

reviewed museum records, including 171 repatriation case reports, and interviewed Smithsonian, Repatriation Review Committee, and tribal officials.

What GAO Recommends

GAO suggests that Congress may wish to consider ways to expedite the Smithsonian's repatriation process, and recommends that the Smithsonian take actions to expand the oversight and reporting role of the special committee, establish an administrative appeals process, and develop a policy for the disposition of culturally unidentifiable items. The Smithsonian agreed with GAO's findings and recommendations.

What GAO Found

Since the NMAI Act was enacted, in 1989, more than 21 years ago, the Smithsonian has offered to repatriate over 5,000 human remains, which account for approximately one-third of the total estimated human remains in its collections. The Smithsonian has also offered to repatriate over 212,000 funerary objects, but the extent of progress is unknown because the Smithsonian has no reliable estimate of the total number of such objects in its collections. The Smithsonian generally makes repatriation decisions based on detailed case reports, and had completed 171 case reports as of December 31, 2010. Developing these case reports is a lengthy and resource-intensive process, in part because the NMAI Act generally requires the Smithsonian to use the best available scientific and historical documentation to identify the origins of its Indian human remains and funerary objects. The Smithsonian originally estimated that the repatriation process would take about 5 years; however, at the pace that it is progressing, GAO believes it could take several more decades to complete this process.

In response to the special committee requirements of the NMAI Act, the Smithsonian established a Repatriation Review Committee to monitor and review the Natural History Museum's repatriation activities. Although the Smithsonian believes Congress intended to limit the committee's jurisdiction to the Natural History Museum, the statutory language and its legislative history do not support that view. Since it was established, the committee has provided no oversight over the repatriation activities of the American Indian

Museum. In addition, GAO found that neither the Smithsonian nor the committee has provided regular information to Congress on the repatriation progress at the Smithsonian. Although this reporting is not required by the act, given the length of time this process has taken and is expected to take in the future, policymakers do not have information that would keep them apprised of the Smithsonian's repatriation efforts. The committee also hears disputes concerning decisions over the return of human remains and objects, but it does not make binding decisions. Moreover, the Smithsonian has no independent administrative appeals process by which tribes who would like to challenge a repatriation decision can seek recourse, and judicial review of the Smithsonian's repatriation decisions may not be practical.

Through December 31, 2010, the Smithsonian estimates that, of the items it has offered for repatriation, about three-quarters of the Indian human remains (4,330 out of 5,980) and about half of the funerary objects (99,550 out of 212,220) have been repatriated. The remaining items have not been repatriated for various reasons, including tribes' lack of resources and cultural beliefs. Resources needed include staff to work on repatriations and appropriate locations to rebury or house the items. In addition, the Smithsonian has not repatriated approximately 340 human remains and 310 funerary objects because it has determined that they cannot be culturally affiliated with a tribe, and it does not have a policy on the disposition of these items. The lack of such a policy limits the transparency of the Smithsonian's actions in handling culturally unidentifiable items for both tribes and policymakers.

ABBREVIATIONS

NAGPRA Native American Graves Protection and Repatriation Act
NMAI Act National Museum of the American Indian Act

May 25, 2011

The Honorable Daniel K. Akaka
Chairman
Committee on Indian Affairs
United States Senate

The Honorable Edward J. Markey
Ranking Member
Committee on Natural Resources
House of Representatives

The Smithsonian Institution holds a large number of Indian human remains and culturally significant objects as part of its museum collections. These human remains and objects have long been a concern for many Indian tribes and Native Hawaiian communities, who have been determined to provide an appropriate resting place for their ancestors. In 1989, the National Museum of the American Indian Act (NMAI Act) was enacted, in part to address these concerns. Sections 11 and 13 of the act generally require the Smithsonian to (1) inventory the Indian and Native Hawaiian human remains and funerary objects in its possession or control, (2) identify the origins of the Indian and Native Hawaiian human remains and funerary objects using the "best available scientific and historical documentation," and (3) upon request repatriate them to lineal descendants or culturally affiliated Indian tribes and Native Hawaiian organizations.[1] The Smithsonian is to carry out the inventory and identification requirements in consultation and cooperation with traditional Indian religious leaders and government officials of Indian tribes. As originally written, the act did not set a deadline for the completion of these tasks. In addition, section 12 of the act requires the Smithsonian to establish a special committee, which the Smithsonian refers to as the Repatriation Review Committee,[2] to monitor and review the inventory, identification, and return of Indian human remains and funerary objects. In addition to these repatriation provisions, the act also establishes a new Smithsonian museum known as the National Museum of the American Indian under a Board of Trustees. The act provides the Board of Trustees with sole authority to, among other things, dispose of any part of the American Indian Museum's collections, subject to the general policies of the Smithsonian's Board of Regents, the overall governing body of the Smithsonian.[3]

In 1990, about a year after enactment of the NMAI Act, the Native American Graves Protection and Repatriation Act (NAGPRA) was enacted, and it established repatriation requirements for federal agencies and museums that receive federal funding, other than the Smithsonian.[4] The repatriation requirements in NAGPRA were more comprehensive than those in the NMAI Act as originally enacted in 1989. NAGPRA covers additional objects—known as sacred objects and objects of cultural patrimony—and establishes specific deadlines for, among other things, completing inventories.[5] NAGPRA also requires the establishment of a review committee to monitor and review the implementation of the inventory and identification process and repatriation activities. We reported on federal agency compliance with NAGPRA in July 2010.[6] In that report, we found that key federal agencies had not fully complied with NAGPRA because they had not identified all of their NAGPRA items or made cultural affiliations in accordance with the act and its deadlines. We recommended, among other things, that the agencies develop plans to complete their required inventories and summaries and submit such plans to Congress; the agencies generally agreed with our recommendations.

On October 9, 1996, the NMAI Act was amended to expand the types of objects covered by the act and establish deadlines for completing certain activities.[7] In particular, the 1996 amendments add a June 1, 1998, deadline for the completion of inventories required under the original act. The amendments also define the term inventory as "a simple, itemized list that, to the extent practicable, identifies, based upon available information held by the Smithsonian Institution, the geographic and cultural affiliation of the remains and objects." The amendments, however, do not alter the original 1989 requirement to use the "best available scientific and historical documentation" to identify the origins of such remains and objects. The amendments also add a new requirement that the Smithsonian prepare summaries for unassociated funerary objects, sacred objects, and objects of cultural patrimony by December 31, 1996. The summaries are to include, at a minimum, a description of the scope of the collection, kinds of objects included, reference to geographical location, means and period of acquisition, and cultural affiliation, where readily ascertainable. Also, upon request the Smithsonian is to return such objects where cultural affiliation has been established in the summary or where a requesting Indian tribe or Native Hawaiian organization can show cultural affiliation by a preponderance of the evidence.[8]

Table 1 includes the definitions of the five types of Indian items covered by the NMAI Act. The Smithsonian has identified two museums that hold collections subject to the NMAI Act: the American Indian Museum and the National Museum of Natural History. Final repatriation decisions for the American Indian Museum are made by its Board of Trustees; the Secretary of the Smithsonian has delegated responsibility for making final repatriation decisions for the Natural History Museum to the Smithsonian's Under Secretary for Science. You asked us to review the status of the Smithsonian's implementation of the NMAI Act's repatriation provisions. This report addresses (1) the extent to which the Smithsonian has fulfilled its repatriation requirements and what challenges it faces, if any, in fulfilling its requirements;

(2) how the special committee provisions in the NMAI Act have been implemented and the challenges the committee faces, if any, in fulfilling its requirements; and (3) the number of human remains and objects that have been repatriated and the reasons for any that have not.[9]

Table 1. Five Types of Indian Items Covered by the NMAI Act

NMAI Act item	Definition
Human remains	Not defined in the NMAI Act.a
Funerary objects	Objects that, as part of a death rite or ceremony of a culture, are intentionally placed with individual human remains, either at the time of burial or later. 20 U.S.C. § 80q-14(4).
Unassociated funerary objects	Objects that, as a part of the death rite or ceremony of a culture, are reasonably believed to have been placed with individual human remains either at the time of death or later, where the remains are not in the possession or control of [the Smithsonian] and the objects can be identified by a preponderance of the evidence as related to specific individuals or families or to known human remains or, by a preponderance of the evidence, as having been removed from a specific burial site of an individual culturally affiliated with a particular Indian tribe. 20 U.S.C. § 80q-9a(a); 25 U.S.C. § 3001(3)(B).
Sacred objects	Specific ceremonial objects which are needed by traditional Native American religious leaders for the practice of traditional Native American religions by their present day adherents. 20 U.S.C. § 80q-9a(a); 25 U.S.C. § 3001(3)(C).
Objects of cultural patrimony	Objects having ongoing historical, traditional, or cultural importance central to the Native American group or culture itself, rather than property owned by an individual Native American, and which, therefore, cannot be alienated, appropriated, or conveyed by any individual regardless of whether or not the individual is a member of the Indian tribe or Native Hawaiian organization and such object shall have been considered inalienable by such Native American group at the time the object was separated from such group. 20 U.S.C. § 80q-9a(a); 25 U.S.C. § 3001(3)(D).

Source: NAGPRA and the NMAI Act.

[a]The NAGPRA regulations define this term as the physical remains of the body of a person of Native American ancestry. 43 C.F.R. § 10.2(d)(1).

To determine the extent to which the Smithsonian has fulfilled its repatriation requirements and what challenges it faces, if any, we examined inventories and summaries prepared by the American Indian and the Natural History Museums. We also analyzed repatriation case reports completed by the two museums to compile key information, including the names of the requesting tribes, time frames for completing the reports, and the repatriation recommendations. We interviewed officials from the museums' respective repatriation offices and the Smithsonian's Office of General Counsel on the repatriation process.[10] We interviewed these officials as well as tribal officials to determine any challenges the Smithsonian faces in implementing the NMAI Act's repatriation requirements. We also obtained in writing the Smithsonian's legal views on how it interprets the NMAI Act and an additional memorandum regarding its legal views.[11]

To determine how the Smithsonian has implemented the requirement to establish a special committee and what challenges the committee faces, if any, we examined the NMAI Act's requirements as well as the Review Committee's charter and bylaws. We examined the comments made by Review Committee members on repatriation case reports; attended portions of two Review Committee meetings in Washington, D.C.; and interviewed six of the seven Review Committee members.[12] Because the Board of Trustees has performed oversight of the American Indian Museum's collections, we interviewed 5 of the 23 board members who were available to meet in between sessions of a board meeting, 4 of the 8 who make up the American Indian Museum Board of Trustees' Repatriation Committee, and received written comments from the full board. For the first and second objectives we also reviewed (1) the American Indian and the Natural History Museums' Repatriation Office progress reports to the Board of Trustees and Review Committee, respectively, and (2) Review Committee annual reports to the Secretary of the Smithsonian, meeting minutes, and other documents to obtain information on implementation.

To determine how many Indian human remains and objects have been repatriated and reasons for any that have not been repatriated, we analyzed museum data as well as specific lists prepared by the museums of the human remains and objects in their collection that were offered for repatriation but not yet repatriated. We contacted 14 of the 68 tribes to which these human remains and objects were culturally affiliated—8 for the American Indian Museum and 6 for the Natural History Museum—and interviewed 5 of them to determine why the items offered had not been repatriated. The other 9 tribes that we contacted did not respond to our inquiries. We chose these tribes based on their geographic location and the number of items offered for repatriation. A more detailed description of our scope and methodology is presented in appendix I.

We conducted this performance audit from July 2010 to May 2011 in accordance with generally accepted government auditing standards. Those standards require that we plan and perform the audit to obtain sufficient, appropriate evidence to provide a reasonable basis for our findings and conclusions based on our audit objectives. We believe that the evidence obtained provides a reasonable basis for our findings and conclusions based on our audit objectives.

BACKGROUND

The Smithsonian Institution was founded in 1846 and is the world's largest museum and research complex, consisting of 19 museums and galleries, the National Zoological Park, and nine research facilities. Of the 137 million artifacts, works of art, and specimens in the Smithsonian's collections, about 126 million are held by the Natural History Museum and about 825,000 are held by the American Indian Museum. Pursuant to the NMAI Act, the American Indian Museum's collection was transferred to the Smithsonian from the former Museum of the American Indian in New York City, founded by George Gustav Heye, and contains items from North America, South America, Central America, and the Caribbean. After the NMAI Act was enacted, in 1989, the American Indian Museum officially assumed control of the Heye collection in June 1990, and the collection was physically moved from New York to a newly constructed cultural resources center near Washington, D.C., from 1999 to 2004. The new American Indian Museum in Washington, D.C., opened its doors to the public in 2004.

The Smithsonian has acquired a large number of Indian human remains and culturally significant objects through a variety of means. For example, in the late 1800s, the Surgeon General of the Army requested U.S. military forces to send thousands of Indian human remains from battlefields and burial sites for the purposes of conducting a cranial study. As a result, thousands of sets of human remains were sent to the Army Medical Museum and then later were transferred to the Smithsonian.[13] Other human remains and many more objects have been collected through archaeological excavations and donations.

According to museum officials, when new collections are acquired, the Smithsonian assigns an identification number—referred to as a catalog number—to each item or set of items at the time of the acquisition or, in some cases, many years later. A single catalog number may include one or more human bones, bone fragments, or objects, and it may include the remains of one or more individuals. All of this information is stored in the museums' electronic catalog system, which is partly based on historical paper card catalogs. Generally, each catalog number in the electronic catalog system includes basic information on the item or set of items, such as a brief description of the item, where the item was collected, and when it was taken into the museum's collection.

Since the NMAI Act was enacted, the Smithsonian has identified approximately 19,780 catalog numbers that potentially include Indian human remains (about 19,150 within the Natural History Museum collections and about 630 within the American Indian Museum collections).[14] This number has changed over time as the museums have either cataloged more human remains or identified additional catalog numbers that contain human remains. According to museum officials, Indian human remains, funerary objects, and other objects potentially subject to repatriation are generally organized within the following museum collections:

- *Physical anthropology* (Natural History Museum only): This collection consists mostly of human remains but, in rare instances, also some funerary objects.
- *Archaeology:* This collection consists of a wide variety of objects, including funerary objects, some human remains, and some potential sacred objects and objects of cultural patrimony.
- *Ethnology:* This collection consists of a wide variety of objects, including potential sacred objects and objects of cultural patrimony, and some human remains and funerary objects.

Museum Missions and Repatriation Offices

The Smithsonian's overall mission is the increase and diffusion of knowledge, and the American Indian and Natural History Museums implement this overall mission in different ways. The American Indian Museum's mission is advancing knowledge and understanding of the Native cultures of the Western Hemisphere, past, present, and future, through partnership with Native people and others. The Natural History Museum's mission is to inspire curiosity, discovery, and learning about nature and culture through outstanding research, collections, exhibitions, and education, but does not specifically refer to partnership with Native people.

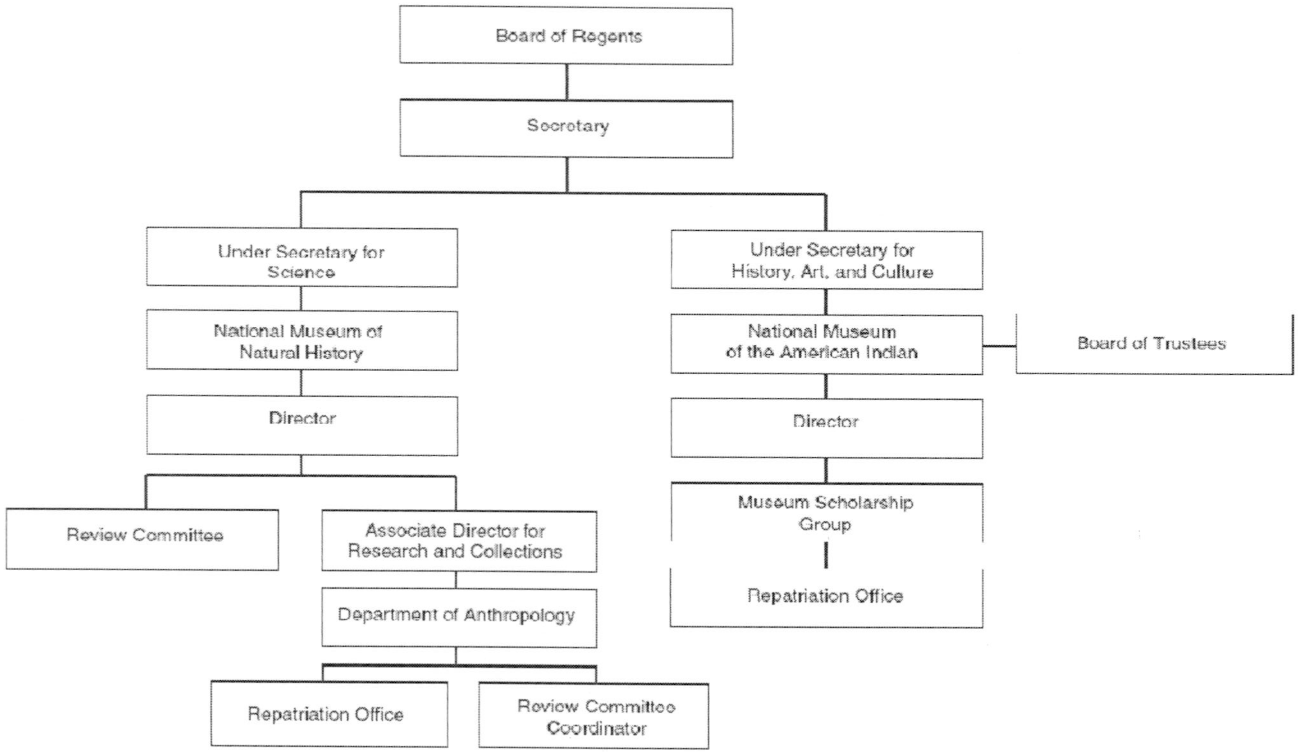

Source: Smithsonian documents and officials, and the NMAI Act.

Figure 1. Organization Chart for the Key Entities Involved in the Smithsonian's Repatriation Efforts.

Both museums have established repatriation offices to carry out their repatriation activities (see figure 1); the American Indian Museum established an office in November 1993 and the Natural History Museum established an office in September 1991. The repatriation offices within the two museums are independent of each other and have separate staffs and budgets. For fiscal year 2010, the American Indian Museum's Repatriation Office had a budget of approximately $580,000 and consisted of five staff—a program manager, repatriation coordinator, and three case officers.[15] In the same fiscal year, the Natural History Museum's Repatriation Office had a budget of approximately $1.7 million (including funding for the Review Committee) and consisted of 11 staff—including a program manager, three case officers, and a lab director with six technical staff.

NAGPRA Requirements and How They Differ from Those of the NMAI Act

One of the purposes of the 1996 amendments to the NMAI Act was to ensure that the requirements for the inventory, identification, and repatriation of human remain and objects in the Smithsonian's possession are being carried out in a manner consistent with NAGPRA.[16] NAGPRA requires each federal agency and museum with NAGPRA items in its collections to (1) compile an inventory of Native American human remains and associated funerary objects; (2) compile a summary of Native American unassociated funerary objects, sacred objects, and objects of cultural patrimony; and (3) repatriate culturally affiliated human remains and objects identified through the inventory or summary processes if the terms and conditions prescribed in the act are met. NAGPRA required that the inventories be completed no later than 5 years after its enactment—by November 16, 1995—and that the summaries be completed no later than 3 years after its enactment—by November 16, 1993. NAGPRA included a provision that allows museums that made a good faith effort to carry out an inventory and identification to apply for an extension of the inventory completion deadline. With respect to inventories, NAGPRA requires that they be completed in consultation with tribal government officials, Native Hawaiian organization officials, and traditional religious leaders. Furthermore, in the inventory, federal agencies and museums are required to identify geographic and cultural affiliation to the extent possible based on information in their possession. If a federal agency or museum determined cultural affiliation for human remains and associated funerary objects to a tribe(s) in an inventory, the act requires it to notify the affected tribe(s) no later than 6 months after the completion of the inventory. The agency or museum is also required to provide a copy of each notice to the Secretary of the Interior for publication in the *Federal Register*. NAGPRA and its implementing regulations generally require that, upon the request of an Indian tribe or Native Hawaiian organization, all culturally affiliated NAGPRA items be returned to the applicable Indian tribe or Native Hawaiian organization expeditiously—within 90 days of receiving the repatriation request but no sooner than 30 days after publication of the notice. However, as we reported in 2010, we found examples where agency officials treated inventories like summaries in that the consultation occurred and cultural affiliation determinations were made after the preparation of the inventory.[17] One of the purposes of the 1996 amendments to the NMAI Act was to ensure that the requirements for the inventory, identification, and repatriation of human remains and objects in the Smithsonian's possession are being carried out in a manner consistent with NAGPRA, but there remain some differences between the two laws. For example, the 1996 amendments to the NMAI Act adopt NAGPRA's definition of inventory, but they do not alter the original 1989 requirement to use the "best available scientific and historical documentation" in identifying the origins of the Indian human remains and funerary objects.[18] In addition, the NMAI Act does not contain specific deadlines for notifying culturally affiliated tribes or returning culturally affiliated human remains. Instead, the NMAI Act requires that culturally affiliated tribes be notified "at the earliest opportunity" and that culturally affiliated items be returned "expeditiously." Some examples of differences between the two acts are summarized in table 2.

Special Committee Requirements under the NMAI Act

Section 12 of the NMAI Act requires the Smithsonian to establish a special committee, which the Smithsonian calls the Repatriation Review Committee (referred to hereafter as the Review Committee), and tasks the committee with, for example,

- ensuring fair and objective consideration and assessment of all relevant evidence with respect to the inventory and identification process;
- reviewing any finding relating to the origin or the return of remains or objects, upon request; and

- facilitating the resolution of any dispute with respect to the return of remains or objects.

Section 12 lays out other requirements with respect to the Review Committee. For example, it requires the Secretary of the Smithsonian to certify by report to Congress at the conclusion of the work of the committee. It also requires the Secretary to provide administrative support for the committee. The Smithsonian established a charter for the Review Committee, which states that the purpose of the committee is to serve in an advisory capacity to the Secretary of the Smithsonian in matters concerning the repatriation of human remains, funerary objects, sacred objects, and objects of cultural patrimony. The charter also discusses the functions of the committee, duties of its members, and rules of evidence, among other things.

Board of Trustees' Authority Established by the NMAI Act

The NMAI Act provides the Board of Trustees of the American Indian Museum with certain authority over the museum's collections. For example, the act states that the Board of Trustees has sole authority, subject to the general policies of the Smithsonian's Board of Regents, to lend, exchange, sell, or otherwise dispose of any part of the collections of the American Indian Museum. The act also states that nothing in section 11 of the act—which addresses inventories—shall be interpreted as limiting the authority of the Smithsonian to return or repatriate Indian human remains and funerary objects. Furthermore, the 1996 amendments to the NMAI Act add that nothing in the summary section may be construed to prevent the Smithsonian from making an inventory or preparing a written summary or carrying out the repatriation of unassociated funerary objects, sacred objects, or objects of cultural patrimony in a manner that exceeds the requirements of the NMAI Act. Based on the flexibilities provided by the NMAI Act, the American Indian Museum established a repatriation policy that differs from the Natural History Museum's and the act's basic repatriation requirements. Under the policy, for example, the American Indian Museum will repatriate items if there is sufficient evidence to establish a "reasonable belief" of cultural affiliation—a lower threshold than the NMAI Act's basic requirement to repatriate items where cultural affiliation can be established by a "preponderance of the evidence."[19] Also, the policy states that the American Indian Museum will take into consideration repatriation requests from non-federally recognized tribes, which are not covered by the NMAI Act's repatriation requirements.

Table 2. Examples of Differences between NAGPRA and the NMAI Act

Topic	NAGPRA	NMAI Act
Information to use in making cultural affiliation determinations for human remains and funerary objects	To the extent possible based on information possessed by the museum or federal agency, identify the geographical and cultural affiliations of Native American human remains and associated funerary objects. 25 U.S.C. § 3003(a).	Using the best available scientific and historical documentation, identify the origins of Indian human remains and funerary objects. 20 U.S.C. § 80q-9(a)(1)(B). Inventory is defined as a simple, itemized list that, to the extent practicable, identifies, based upon available information held by the Smithsonian Institution, the eographic and cultural affiliations of the remains and objects. 20 U.S.C. § 80q-9(a)(3).
Retaining certain items for scientific study	Federal agencies and museums shall expeditiously return requested culturally affiliated [NAGPRA items] unless such items are indispensable for completion of a specific scientific study, the outcome of which would be of major benefit to the United States. Such items shall be returned no later than 90 days after the date on which the scientific study is completed. 25 U.S.C. § 3005(b).	The NMAI Act does not refer to retaining certain items for scientific study.
Competing claims	Where there are multiple requests for repatriation of [NAGPRA items] and, after complying with the applicable requirements, the federal agency or museum cannot clearly determine which requesting party is the most appropriate claimant, the agency or museum may retain such item until the requesting parties agree upon its disposition or the dispute is otherwise resolved pursuant to NAGPRA or by a federal court. 25 U.S.C. § 3005(e).	The NMAI Act does not address what the Smithsonian should do when there are competing claims.

Topic	NAGPRA	NMAI Act
Annual reports to Congress by the Review Committee	The Review Committee established under NAGPRA is required to submit an annual report to Congress. 25 U.S.C. § 3006(h).	At the conclusion of the work of the special committee established under the NMAI Act, the Secretary of the Smithsonian shall so certify by report to Congress. 20 U.S.C. § 80q-10(f).
Federal Advisory Committee Acta	The Review Committee established under NAGPRA is subject to the Federal Advisory Committee Act.	The special committee established under the NMAI Act is exempt from the Federal Advisory Committee Act. 20 U.S.C. § 80q-10(g). This means it is not required to meet the act's requirements, such as the requirement to hold public meetings.
Private cause of action for alleged violations	NAGPRA creates a private cause of action, which allows lawsuits to be brought in federal court in response to alleged violations. 25 U.S.C. § 3013.	Nothing in the NMAI Act authorizes a private cause of action.

Source: NAGPRA and the NMAI Act.

[a]Pub. L. No. 92-463, 86 Stat. 770 (1972) (classified at 5 U.S.C. app. 2).

Since 1989, the Smithsonian Has Prepared Required Summaries and Inventories and Has Offered to Repatriate about One-Third of Its Indian Human Remains

The American Indian and Natural History Museums generally prepared summaries and inventories within the deadlines established in the NMAI Act, but their inventories and the process they used to prepare them raise questions about their compliance with some of the statutory requirements.

Since 1989, the Smithsonian estimates that it has offered to repatriate the Indian human remains in about one-third of the catalog numbers identified as possibly including human remains.

Smithsonian officials that we spoke with identified challenges that the museums face in carrying out their repatriation requirements under the NMAI Act.

Both Museums Generally Prepared Required Documents on Time, but Inventories Raise Questions about Compliance with the NMAI Act

The American Indian and Natural History Museums generally prepared required documents by the deadlines established in the NMAI Act. The American Indian Museum prepared its first set of inventories in 1993. In an effort to voluntarily follow NAGPRA's more comprehensive requirements, it included its entire collection in these inventories—not just the human remains and funerary objects it was required to inventory at the time. Museum officials later found that the 1993 inventory did not include an additional 5,000 catalog numbers containing objects. These catalog numbers had never been entered into the museum's electronic catalog, which was the primary source for the 1993 inventories. As a result, the museum prepared additional inventories in 1995 covering these 5,000 catalog numbers. The museum provided all federally recognized tribes with inventories of the collections that could be affiliated to them.[20] After the enactment of the 1996 amendments, the museum did not revise its inventories or prepare separate summaries because officials believed that the museum had already complied with the new requirements.

The Natural History Museum also generally prepared its summary and inventory documents by the statutory deadlines.

- The museum prepared 171 summaries of its ethnological collection from the United States based on information in its electronic catalog—170 by tribal grouping and 1 for items that could not be associated with any tribal group. Of these 171 summaries, 116 were prepared by the December 31, 1996, deadline established by the 1996 amendments,[21] 50 were completed within 2 months of the deadline, and 5 were completed still later. Some of these summaries were prepared prior to the 1996 amendments' enactment, since the museum had prepared summaries upon request from tribes in an effort to voluntarily follow NAGPRA's requirement to prepare summaries. After the 1996 amendments were enacted, the museum provided all federally recognized tribes with summaries of the collections that could be affiliated to them.
- The museum also prepared 64 inventories of its physical anthropology and archaeology collections from the United States—13 for Alaska regions, 1 for each additional state and the District of Columbia, and 1 for items that could not be associated with a particular state. These

inventories identified about 16,000 catalog numbers as possibly including human remains and, according to the museum's Repatriation Office, about 3,000 catalog numbers as possibly including funerary objects.[22] According to museum officials, these inventories provided specific geographic information for most human remains and, in some cases, specific information about the possible cultural affiliations of the human remains and funerary objects. The Natural History Museum prepared all of its inventories by the June 1, 1998, deadline and provided all federally recognized tribes with inventories of the collections that could be affiliated to them. As with the American Indian Museum, the inventories prepared by the Natural History Museum included potentially many more items than the human remains and funerary objects required by the NMAI Act enacted in 1989. For example, the inventories included the museum's entire archaeology collection from the United States, which consisted of over 200,000 catalog numbers containing over 1 million objects.

Although both museums generally prepared their summaries and inventories by the statutory deadlines, the process for preparing the inventories raises questions about compliance with two of the NMAI Act's requirements. The first question is the extent to which the museums prepared their inventories in consultation and cooperation with traditional Indian religious leaders and government officials of Indian tribes, as required by the NMAI Act. Section 11 directs the Secretary of the Smithsonian, in consultation and cooperation with traditional Indian religious leaders and government officials of Indian tribes, to inventory the Indian human remains and funerary objects in the possession or control of the Smithsonian and, using the best available scientific and historical documentation, identify the origins of such remains and objects. The 1996 amendments did not alter this language, although they added a definition of inventory. However, the Smithsonian generally began the consultation process with Indian tribes after the inventories from both museums were distributed. The second question is the extent to which the Natural History Museum's inventories—which were finalized after the 1996 amendments— identified geographic and cultural affiliations to the extent practicable based on information held by the Smithsonian, as required by the amendments. Its inventories generally identified geographic and cultural affiliations only where such information was readily available in the museum's electronic catalog. In preparing its inventories, the museum did not consult other information that the Smithsonian had in its possession to attempt to identify geographic and cultural affiliations, such as records in the National Anthropological Archives or the Smithsonian Institution Archives, which may have included work papers of collectors and donors. According to the Smithsonian's legal views and Smithsonian documents, this is one of the reasons why the cultural affiliations in the Natural History Museum's inventories were tentative.

In its legal views, however, the Smithsonian states that it has fully complied with the statutory requirements for preparing inventories. First, the Smithsonian states that the statutory language does not require that consultation occur prior to the inventory being completed. The Smithsonian points to the definition of inventory added by the 1996 amendments in support of its interpretation, noting that one could easily construe the consultation requirement to apply with greater force to the requirement to use the best available scientific and historical documentation to identify the origins of the human remains and objects rather than to the development of the inventories.[23] Second, the Smithsonian states that the law allows the Smithsonian to determine, for itself, what was practicable in order to meet the statutory deadline for completion of the inventories. The Smithsonian acknowledges that neither the American Indian nor the Natural History Museum reviewed each and every source maintained by the Smithsonian for preparing the inventories—including the National Anthropological Archives or individual staff files—because accessing those sources would not have been practicable given the size and scope of the Smithsonian's collection.

Furthermore, according to the Smithsonian's legal views, the Smithsonian does not interpret section 11 as necessarily requiring that the inventory and identification process occur simultaneously, and therefore it has adopted a two-step process to fulfill section 11's requirements. The first step is to prepare a detailed listing (the inventory) of the human remains and funerary objects in each museum's collection using information in the electronic catalog. The Smithsonian stated that it does not believe that the NMAI Act—either as originally enacted or after the 1996 amendments— requires cultural affiliations included in the inventories to necessarily be conclusive and dispositive. The second step is to prepare repatriation case reports (the identification). During the second step, the museums generally consult with tribes and consider all relevant information, including information held by the Smithsonian as well as other information needed to meet the NMAI Act's requirement that the Smithsonian use the best available scientific and historic documentation to identify the origins of remains and funerary objects, according to officials. Generally, each case report prepared by the museums includes a determination of cultural affiliation and a recommendation regarding repatriation, according to officials. The officials told us that the museums generally undertake the second step only after a tribe submits a repatriation claim based on information in the inventories.[24]

The legislative history of the 1996 amendments provides little clear guidance concerning the meaning of section 11.[25] The congressional committee report accompanying the 1996 amendments notes that the amendments were entirely consistent with the Smithsonian's then-current administrative practice and adopted the Smithsonian's administrative deadline of June 1, 1998, to complete an inventory of Indian human remains and funerary objects in its possession. This suggests that the 1996 amendments ratified the Smithsonian's two-step approach to inventory and identification. The committee report, however, also notes that one intent of the amendments was to ensure that the requirements for the inventory, identification, and repatriation of human remains and funerary objects in the possession of the Smithsonian was being carried out in a manner consistent with NAGPRA, which suggests that the Smithsonian should have included geographic and cultural affiliations in its inventory to the extent practicable based on information held by the Smithsonian.

Had the Smithsonian implemented the latter interpretation, it would have faced serious challenges in conducting the required consultations and research necessary to make the required cultural affiliations within the statutory deadlines, given the resources devoted to the task. Natural History Museum staff told us that they could not have reviewed all relevant information when preparing the inventories because they did not have time to do so by the deadline. We recognize the dilemma that the Smithsonian faced; it had to either prepare incomplete inventories by the deadline or prepare complete inventories and miss the deadline. Either approach would have resulted in questions about compliance with the NMAI Act. In addition, Smithsonian officials believe that only the first step of the two-step process was required to be completed within the deadline. Therefore, under this interpretation, the Smithsonian does not have a statutory deadline to complete the remaining consultations and make the remaining cultural affiliation determinations. The congressional committee reports accompanying the 1989 act indicate that the Smithsonian estimated that the identification and inventory of Indian human remains as well as notification of affected tribes and return of the remains and funerary objects would take 5 years.[26] However, more than 21 years later, these efforts are still under way.

Smithsonian's Progress in Offering Human Remains and Objects for Repatriation Has Been Slow

From the passage of the NMAI Act in 1989 through December 2010, the Smithsonian estimates that it has offered to repatriate the Indian human remains in approximately one-third (about 5,280) of the estimated 19,780 catalog numbers identified as possibly including Indian human remains since the act was passed.[27] The American Indian Museum offered to repatriate human remains in about 40 percent (about 250) of its estimated 630 catalog numbers. The Natural History Museum has offered to repatriate human remains in about 25 percent (about 5,040) of its estimated 19,150 catalog numbers containing Indian human remains.

Table 3. Estimated Number of Indian Human Remains and Objects Offered for Repatriation as of December 31, 2010

	Human remains		Funerary objects		Sacred objects and objects of cultural patrimony	
Museum	Estimated catalog numbers	Estimated actual numbers[a]	Estimated catalog numbers	Estimated actual numbers	Estimated catalog numbers	Estimated actual numbers
American Indian	250	420	980	29,400[b]	1,040	1,190
Natural History	5,040	5,560	2,470	182,820	10	50
Total	**5,280**	**5,980**	**3,460**	**212,220**	**1,050**	**1,240**

Source: GAO analysis of data provided by the Smithsonian's American Indian and Natural History Museums.

Notes: Because the numbers provided in this table are estimates, we have rounded them to the nearest ten. Therefore, totals may not add because of rounding.

[a]The American Indian Museum currently calculates the minimum number of individuals, but previously used other methods, including counts of individual elements, counts of the number of bone fragments, and other counting standards. The minimum number of individuals cannot be estimated for human remains that were repatriated before the counting method was standardized.

[b]The American Indian Museum's Repatriation Manager said that some of these are lots rather than individual items. A lot generally is a group of human remains or artifacts that are related in some way, but are not individually numbered or identified.

The Smithsonian has also offered to repatriate more than 212,000 funerary objects from about 3,460 catalog numbers and about 1,240 sacred objects and objects of cultural patrimony from about 1,050 catalog numbers through 2010 (see table 3). We could not determine what share of the total this represents because the Smithsonian cannot provide a reliable estimate of the number of funerary objects in its collections and, for sacred objects and objects of cultural patrimony, the Smithsonian relies on tribes to assist in identifying such objects.[28] The Smithsonian generally makes repatriation decisions based on the case reports prepared by case officers at each museum. At the Natural History Museum, the Secretary of the Smithsonian has delegated authority for making decisions to the Under Secretary for Science; at the American Indian Museum the decision is made by the Board of Trustees. Through December 31, 2010, case officers had completed 76 case reports at the American Indian Museum and 95 at the Natural History Museum.[29] Case reports vary in scope and complexity, and therefore the length of time necessary to complete them varies. Both museums' Repatriation Managers provided estimates for how long case reports should take to complete (18 months for the American Indian Museum, on average, and at least 1 year for the Natural History Museum), but added that time frames can vary greatly depending on the circumstances. Also, they said that these estimates are based on a starting point of when a case officer begins to actively work on a case report. Therefore, their estimates do not include the months or years during which claims may be pending awaiting active consideration. We found that it took a median of 2.4 years for the Smithsonian to complete a case report from the date of an official claim letter to the date of a case report. This varied from 1 month to 18.3 years. Appendix II provides details on the length of time taken by the museums to respond to repatriation claims. According to the Smithsonian's legal views, case reports need to be detailed in order to meet both the act's statutory requirements and the Smithsonian's fiduciary duties. Under the Smithsonian's legal views, the Smithsonian has an affirmative obligation to prepare inventories and to use the best available scientific and historical documentation to identify the origins of such remains and funerary objects. Accordingly, Smithsonian officials told us that once they had addressed all of the pending requests, they would begin culturally affiliating the human remains and objects still in their collections. In preparing case reports, case officers generally review relevant documentation, including relevant information held by the Smithsonian, and consult with tribes. While the Smithsonian sometimes holds the best available information about its collections, according to officials, case officers sometimes review sources held outside of the Smithsonian as well, such as articles published in journals, state site files, and relevant archival information. In some cases, case officers have traveled to archives across the country to review relevant information, such as notes taken by collectors in the field, according to the

Natural History Museum's Repatriation Manager. The slow progress can be attributed, in part, to the Smithsonian's view that it has a legal and fiduciary duty to use the best available scientific and historical documentation to determine the cultural affiliation of human remains and objects.[30] The two museums have established internal goals for the number of case reports they will complete in 2011—5 at the Natural History Museum and 4 at the American Indian Museum. However, Smithsonian officials could not estimate when they will complete this process for human remains and funerary objects. At the pace the Smithsonian has been going, it could take decades more to prepare case reports for the remaining human remains and funerary objects in its collections.

The Smithsonian Identified Challenges to Meeting Its Repatriation Requirements

Officials we spoke with from the Smithsonian, the Review Committee, and the American Indian Museum's Board of Trustees identified challenges the museums face in carrying out the Smithsonian's repatriation requirements under the NMAI Act. These challenges fall into four main categories:

- *Limited staff and staff turnover:* For example, the Board of Trustees told us that the American Indian Museum's Repatriation Office is small and has suffered over the years from turnover and vacancies. The Natural History Museum's Repatriation Manager said that the museum had limited staff to prepare repatriation case reports, which has contributed to the length of time needed to address claims. According to the American Indian Museum's Repatriation Manager, in one instance the museum was not permitted to fill an open position for a repatriation staff member because of budgetary constraints, and this resulted in over a year of lost research time.
- *Complex or limited information:* Repatriation staff told us that complex and sometimes limited records of the Smithsonian's collections can pose a challenge. For example, the Natural History Museum's Repatriation Manager told us that records for late 19th and early 20th century archaeological excavations are often incomplete and scattered among record locations at the museum. Furthermore, the manager told us that some collections have been transferred between the Natural History Museum and non-Smithsonian museums and that,

in some cases, relevant information in the original records was omitted or simplified during the transfer of items. The American Indian Museum's Repatriation Manager also told us that complex and sometimes limited records of the Smithsonian's collections can pose a challenge, but added that the museum lacks information on the origin of only a few human remains and funerary objects in its collections.

- *Difficulties overcoming tribal issues:* Review Committee and board officials said that tribes' limited resources for repatriation activities and turnover in tribal governments can pose challenges. Furthermore, the Review Committee has repeatedly expressed its concerns about whether the Natural History Museum's repatriation staff are doing enough to reach out to tribes. The committee has recommended several times between 2003 and 2010 that the museum's Repatriation Office hire a tribal liaison to conduct tribal outreach. The Repatriation Manager said, however, that a tribal liaison is not needed because repatriation staff conduct outreach and have built positive relationships with tribes.
- *Poor data management* (American Indian Museum): The American Indian Museum has historically not maintained centralized files related to its repatriation activities, according to the museum's Repatriation Manager. Instead, staff members at that museum have kept their own separate working files. As a result, repatriation staff have faced difficulties in locating case-related information. To tackle this challenge, the American Indian Museum adopted a new case management system in January 2011 to better organize and track its repatriation activities. The new system will allow the museum to store extensive amounts of case-related data in a centralized system and, for example, allow the museum to more quickly respond to inquiries about repatriation cases, according to the museum's Repatriation Manager.

The Review Committee's Oversight and Reporting Are Limited, and It Faces Some Challenges to Fulfilling Its Requirements

The Review Committee conducts numerous activities to implement the special committee provisions in the NMAI Act, but we found its oversight and reporting are limited, and it faces some challenges in fulfilling its requirements under the NMAI Act. Contrary to the NMAI Act, the Review Committee does not monitor and review the American Indian Museum's inventory, identification, and repatriation activities, although it does monitor and review the Natural History Museum's inventory, identification, and repatriation activities. The Review Committee also does not submit reports to Congress on the progress of repatriation activities at the Smithsonian. In addition, although the Review Committee has heard few disputes, no independent appeals process exists to challenge the Smithsonian's cultural affiliation and repatriation decisions. Finally, the Review Committee identified challenges it faces in fulfilling its requirements under the NMAI Act.

Contrary to the NMAI Act, the Review Committee Only Monitors the Repatriation Activities of the Natural History Museum

Section 12 of the NMAI Act requires the Secretary of the Smithsonian to appoint a special committee to monitor and review the inventory, identification, and return of Indian human remains and objects under the act. The law does not limit the applicability of the Review Committee to the Natural History Museum. The Secretary nevertheless established a Review Committee to meet this requirement in 1990 that oversees only the Natural History Museum's repatriation activities and is housed within that museum. According to the Smithsonian's legal views, it interprets the act as limiting the Review Committee's oversight of repatriation activities to the Natural History Museum's repatriation activities. The Smithsonian's five reasons for its position, along with our response, are presented below.

- *The NMAI Act only covered items that the Smithsonian had at the time of enactment in 1989:* The Smithsonian's legal views are that Congress only intended the Review Committee to advise the Smithsonian with respect to the collection of Indian human remains and funerary objects in the possession of the Smithsonian at the time of the NMAI Act's enactment in 1989. At that time, all such items were all in the collections of the Natural History Museum. The Smithsonian bases this interpretation on the statutory language and a congressional committee report that said one purpose of the act was to provide a process of identification for the human remains of Native

Americans that are currently in the possession of the Smithsonian Institution.[31] However, the version of the act that this report accompanied did not become law. The congressional committee report accompanying the version of the act that became law notes that the Smithsonian is to complete an inventory of Indian human remains and funerary objects in the Smithsonian collections which, in due course, will encompass those in the existing Heye collection.[32] Furthermore, section 12 and the act's legislative history do not indicate that the Review Committee's jurisdiction is limited to the Natural History Museum, nor do they include any language that would dictate a time when the committee's jurisdiction should begin. The language of section 12 clearly directs the Secretary to appoint a special committee to monitor and review the inventory, identification, and return of Indian human remains and objects under the NMAI Act.

- *The Review Committee provision in section 12 of the NMAI Act does not address the Heye collection:* The Smithsonian's legal views are that Congress neither addressed nor considered whether the Review Committee's jurisdiction should extend to human remains and funerary objects obtained through the transfer of the Heye collection because at the time the Smithsonian was not aware that the collection contained human remains or funerary objects. However, the act's legislative history demonstrates that Congress believed the collection contained human remains and funerary objects because it discussed an inventory of the human remains and funerary objects in the Heye collection in the congressional committee report accompanying the version of the act that became law.
- *The American Indian Museum did not exist at the time of enactment:* Since the American Indian Museum did not exist at the time of the act's enactment in 1989, the Smithsonian's legal view is that it did not have any collections that could be subject to the act's repatriation provisions. However, 6 months before the act's passage, the Museum of the American Indian in New York and the Smithsonian entered into a memorandum of understanding to transfer the museum's assets to the Smithsonian. When Congress passed the NMAI Act in 1989, it knew that the new American Indian Museum would house the Heye collection. Moreover, the act established the American Indian Museum and therefore it existed as of the date the law was enacted.
- *The American Indian Museum did not exist when the Review Committee began its work:* Because the Review Committee by statute

was to begin its repatriation review process within 120 days of the act's passage, the Smithsonian's legal view is that Congress could not have intended its charge to extend to the American Indian Museum's collection since the museum did not exist 120 days after the act's passage. However, section 12 only required the Secretary to appoint the Review Committee 120 days after the act's passage; section 12 is silent as to when the committee was to begin its work. Moreover, as stated above, the act established the American Indian Museum and therefore it existed as of the date the law was enacted.

- *The NMAI Act provides the Board of Trustees with sole authority over the museum's collections:* The Smithsonian's legal view is that by granting the American Indian Museum Board of Trustees sole authority over the museum's new collection, Congress intended for the board to have independent, plenary authority over its collections, subject only to the general policies of the Board of Regents. In the Smithsonian's legal view, given this intention, Congress would not have provided the Board of Trustees with such broad powers, and, at the same time, cause it to be subject to the oversight of an independent review committee. We asked Smithsonian officials to provide examples of how the Review Committee would interfere with the Board of Trustees' sole authority if the committee reviewed the American Indian Museum case reports and heard disputes, but none were provided. We therefore believe that the Review Committee's monitoring and review of the American Indian Museum's repatriation activities would not interfere with the board's sole authority over the museum's collections and, in particular, its policies to repatriate to non-federally recognized tribes and to make cultural affiliations using a "reasonable basis" standard. This is because the Review Committee's role is only advisory, as acknowledged by the Smithsonian.

Even though the Review Committee has not been overseeing the repatriation activities of the American Indian Museum, since its establishment its Board of Trustees has overseen repatriation activities and has taken an active role in the repatriation process. For example, in 1991, the board adopted a repatriation policy that assigned specific authority and responsibility for each aspect of the repatriation process. It has also overseen the activities of the museum's own Repatriation Office at board meetings. For example, board members told us they review and comment on repatriation case reports, vote to approve each report, sometimes contribute to case reports, and have been involved in inventorying museum collections. In addition, the board has, at times, created a Repatriation Committee composed of a subset of board members to further its oversight of the museum's repatriation program. No dispute had been presented to the board for resolution through December 31, 2010, but in 2009 it did help resolve a challenge to a repatriation recommendation.[33] Should there be a dispute in the future, the board told us that it plans to rely on its recently adopted process for initiating an ad hoc Special Review Committee to resolve disputes. The process states that a Special Review Committee would be convened by the board's Repatriation Committee.

The Review Committee Monitors the Natural History Museum but Does Not Report to Congress

To fulfill its responsibility under the NMAI Act to monitor and review the inventory, identification, and return of Indian human remains and objects, the Review Committee has performed a number of activities to oversee the Natural History Museum's repatriation process including the following:

- *Assessing the Natural History Museum's progress in implementing the act:* The committee generally meets twice annually with Repatriation Office staff and sometimes with other museum staff, including management, to discuss the status of ongoing claims and other repatriation activities. During the meetings, case officers report their interactions with tribes as they address the tribes' claims for the repatriation of objects or human remains. The meetings also allow committee members to review candidates to fill vacant committee seats, discuss the status of personnel in the Repatriation Office, and raise concerns regarding the repatriation process with the office program manager.
- *Reviewing museum case reports:* The committee's reviews of the Repatriation Office's repatriation case reports are intended to offer an "independent appraisal of whether the case reports provide a fair and objective consideration and assessment of all relevant information," according to the Review Committee annual report. The committee examines the methodology and information the case officers use during their research, assesses their conclusions, and, if necessary,

provides editorial suggestions to clarify and improve the reports. The committee has been provided courtesy copies of some case reports prepared by the American Indian Museum's Repatriation Office.

- *Reporting annually to the Secretary:* The committee's reports include concerns it has regarding the repatriation process at the Natural History Museum and updates on disputes, or potential disputes, over cultural affiliation. The reports also provide information regarding conferences or workshops the committee has attended or organized and coordination efforts, if any, the Review Committee has had with the American Indian Museum.
- *Hearing and helping resolve disputes:* The committee hears disputes brought by tribes and other interested parties regarding repatriation decisions by the Natural History Museum and makes recommendations for resolving these disputes to the Secretary of the Smithsonian. It has heard two such disputes, which we describe later in this report. In a separate case, the committee reported that it was able to avoid a potential dispute when it arranged a consultation with one tribe in Oregon, other potentially affiliated Oregon tribes, and expert consultants after a tribe complained about a case report that did not recommend repatriation to the tribe. According to the Review Committee, the meeting proved to be extremely helpful and provided new information for the Review Committee to consider. As a result, the Repatriation Office decided to rewrite its report on the remains and reassess its recommendation. The human remains and funerary objects were later found to be culturally affiliated with two tribes.
- *Conducting tribal outreach:* The committee has a long-standing policy of interacting with Native American communities and relevant organizations. For example, committee members have attended NAGPRA Review Committee meetings and conferences to explain the Smithsonian repatriation process to tribes. The committee also provided support for a 1995 repatriation workshop organized by the American Indian Museum and conducted a survey in 2001 of tribes in California to determine their level of interest in having the Natural History Museum's Repatriation Office conduct workshops on Smithsonian repatriation.

Although section 12 of the NMAI Act requires the Secretary, at the conclusion of the work of the Review Committee, to so certify by report to Congress, there is no annual reporting requirement similar to the one required for the NAGPRA Review Committee. As we stated earlier, in 1989, it was estimated that the Smithsonian Review Committee would conclude its work in about 5 years and cease to exist at the end of fiscal year 1995.[34] Yet the committee's monitoring and review of repatriation activities at the Natural History Museum has been ongoing since the committee's establishment in 1990. In fact, the Smithsonian is not required to report annually to Congress outside of the annual budget process, and Smithsonian officials said the Smithsonian has not reported to Congress on repatriation activities on a regular basis since the NMAI Act was enacted.[35] Furthermore, the Board of Trustees of the American Indian Museum does not have a formal reporting process to inform the Secretary of the Smithsonian or the Smithsonian's Board of Regents of its activities. As a result, over the last 21 years, policymakers have not received regular information to assess the effectiveness of the Smithsonian's efforts to repatriate the Indian human remains and objects in its collections. We believe that this would be an appropriate role for the Smithsonian's Review Committee, and would be similar to the role of the NAGPRA Review Committee.

The Review Committee Has Heard Few Disputes, and No Independent Appeals Process Exists for Smithsonian Decisions

As stated above, the Review Committee is also responsible for hearing disputes at the Natural History Museum with respect to the return of Indian human remains or objects and makes nonbinding recommendations to the Secretary of the Smithsonian. Since the Review Committee was established, in 1990, only two disputes have been brought before it.

- In 1995, a tribe disputed the Natural History Museum's Repatriation Office's finding that the human remains and funerary objects it claimed were culturally unidentifiable and recommendation that they be held until the museum could determine their cultural affiliation. The Review Committee reviewed the case report, requested written summaries of the positions of the museum and the tribe, heard testimony presented by the museum and the tribe, and recommended that the human remains be repatriated to the tribe and that other potentially affiliated tribes be notified of the decision. Several of the notified tribes disputed the repatriation recommendation, and the tribes reached an agreement to jointly repatriate the human remains and funerary objects. In the end, the Secretary decided to implement the committee's recommendation and repatriated the remains and funerary objects to the requesting tribe and also to four additional tribes in 1997.

- In 2009, a tribal group disputed the Repatriation Office's finding that two items it had claimed were not culturally affiliated with the tribes within the group, and that there was insufficient evidence to determine that four additional items met the statutory definition of sacred objects and objects of cultural patrimony. The Review Committee again reviewed the case report, requested position statements from the tribal group and the museum, and heard testimony and unanimously agreed that the Natural History Museum's cultural affiliation determination was incorrect for the two items and that all six items met the statutory definition of sacred objects and objects of cultural patrimony. On the basis of its review of this evidence, the Review Committee recommended to the Secretary that the items be offered for repatriation. However, the Under Secretary for Science decided that the group had not presented sufficient evidence to establish by the required legal standard that the items met the statutory definitions or were culturally affiliated with any tribe in the group, so the Smithsonian would retain the items.[36] In the letter informing the group of its decision, the Under Secretary stated that although he respected the Review Committee's recommendation and understood why the committee "may have given more weight to general assertions provided by tribal leaders," the tribal group had not given sufficient evidence to prove its claim.

An official from the tribal group involved in the second dispute told us that the tribal group has considered challenging the Secretary's decision, but it has no recourse because the Smithsonian does not have an appeals process and cannot be sued in federal court for the decision. The American Indian Museum's Board of Trustees, which makes final repatriations decisions for that museum, established an appeals process in 2010 whereby, in the event of a dispute, the board would appoint five individuals to an ad hoc Special Review Committee to hear the dispute. However, this process lacks independence, because it relies on decision makers overseeing their own decisions. The Smithsonian also cannot be sued under the NMAI Act or the Administrative Procedures Act, the law commonly used to sue federal agencies.[37] Currently, the Smithsonian Board of Regents is the only entity within the Smithsonian organization that has the authority to oversee the decisions of both the Secretary and the NMAI Board of Trustees, but there is no existing process to appeal these decisions to the Board of Regents. In contrast, under NAGPRA, tribes can use the Administrative Procedures Act or section 15 of NAGPRA to challenge a federal agency's repatriation decision if they believe it violates the act.

The Review Committee Identified Challenges It Faces

The Review Committee has identified two challenges it faces to implementing its responsibilities under the NMAI Act. First, the Review Committee has documented its inability to oversee the American Indian Museum's repatriation activities as a challenge. The relationship between the Review Committee and the American Indian Museum has been mixed. Since its establishment, the Review Committee has maintained that the NMAI Act mandates a single review committee for monitoring repatriation activities at all museums and units of the Smithsonian Institution. The American Indian and Natural History Museums do coordinate on some issues, such as conducting tribal consultations and providing funding for consultation and repatriation expenses for tribes.[38] However, the American Indian Museum's board has consistently stressed its independence from the Review Committee with regard to monitoring the repatriation process. According to the Review Committee, there has been no direct communication between the committee and the Board of Trustees as of December 31, 2010.

According to the Review Committee's annual reports, it has taken steps to reach out to the American Indian Museum and offer some oversight of its repatriation program. For example, during the late 1990s, the Review Committee's annual reports indicate that the committee requested, received, and reviewed courtesy copies of some American Indian Museum case reports. The committee suggested that the Natural History Museum's Repatriation Office coordinate more closely with the American Indian Museum, along with other Smithsonian museums, and other institutions to help ensure consistency in repatriation policy. The Review Committee also requested that it be much more involved in the American Indian Museum's repatriation process to meet its mandate.

In its 2000 annual report, the committee informed the Secretary that it had met with resistance in trying to monitor the American Indian Museum's repatriation activities, emphasizing its belief that its mandate encompassed the repatriation activities of the museum. The committee further stated that if it could not perform these duties, the American Indian Museum would continue to be "the only museum in the United States that receives federal funding and [is] not subject to a monitoring of its repatriation activities by an independent committee without a direct interest in activities other than repatriation." The Review Committee also reported in 2005 and 2007 that it had conducted little or no monitoring of the American Indian Museum's repatriation activities.

However, dialogue has opened up recently between the two museums, with potential for the relationship to expand, according to the Chair of the Review Committee. Furthermore, according to the Review Committee, the current Directors of the American Indian and Natural History Museums have expressed interest in establishing a more collaborative relationship between the two museums' repatriation programs.

The second challenge identified by the Review Committee is a lack of consistent administrative support. The committee has experienced two lengthy instances during which it did not have a coordinator, a position that handles a variety of tasks, including arranging biannual meetings (travel, reimbursements to members), drafting minutes of the meetings (on which the annual reports to the Secretary are largely based), and managing the process for filling open seats on the committee.

In the first instance, in July 2005, the coordinator resigned and the Review Committee operated without a coordinator until October 2006. In its 2005 annual report, the Review Committee stated its concern over the length of time it took to fill this position and the negative effect that not having administrative support had on its work. For example, the committee stated that without a coordinator, it was not possible for it to prepare formal minutes for meetings in 2006. Instead, a brief outline of the meeting was recorded after a new coordinator was hired in October 2006.

In the second instance, according to the Natural History Museum's Repatriation Manager, the coordinator was released by the Smithsonian in December 2007 because of a reduction in workforce at the Smithsonian. A museum employee was transferred to the coordinator position that same month but later resigned in February 2008, and the Smithsonian did not hire a new coordinator until March 2009, resulting in an additional year without a coordinator. Although the 2007 meeting minutes had been transcribed by the time the new coordinator had been hired, as of December 31, 2010, the coordinator was in the process of preparing the minutes for 2009 and 2010. There are also no minutes for the 2008 meetings, and the recordings for those meetings have not yet been transcribed. The committee has said that not having a coordinator from 2008 to 2009 made it difficult for it to maintain documentation of its activities and make appropriate logistical arrangements necessary for the committee to function. According to Smithsonian officials, during the time that the Review Committee was without a coordinator, its travel, reimbursement, meeting arrangements, and the process for filling open seats were facilitated by museum staff in coordination with the Review Committee. Smithsonian officials added that they offered to pay for transcription of meeting minutes, but the Review Committee decided to wait until a coordinator was in place to transcribe the tapes.

Most Human Remains and Many Objects Offered for Repatriation Have Been Repatriated, but the Smithsonian Has No Policy on Culturally Unidentifiable Items

The Smithsonian estimates that, of the items offered for repatriation, it has repatriated about three-quarters of the Indian human remains, about half of the funerary objects, and almost all the sacred objects and objects of cultural patrimony. Some items have not been repatriated for a variety of reasons, including tribes' lack of resources, cultural beliefs, and tribal government issues. In addition, the Smithsonian has not repatriated some human remains and funerary objects that it has determined to be culturally unidentifiable, and it does not have a policy on how it will undertake the ultimate disposition of these items.

The Smithsonian Estimates That It Has Repatriated About 4,330 Indian Human Remains and About 100,700 Objects

The Smithsonian estimates that, of the items offered for repatriation, as of December 31, 2010, it has repatriated about three-quarters (4,330) of the Indian human remains, about half (99,550) of the funerary objects, and nearly all (1,140) sacred objects and objects of cultural patrimony (see table 4).

Officials from several tribes that we spoke with, that had repatriation experiences with the American Indian and Natural History Museums, expressed overall satisfaction with how the Smithsonian facilitated the return of human remains and objects once offered for repatriation.

Table 4. Estimated Number of Indian Human Remains and Objects Repatriated as of December 31, 2010

	Human remains[a]			Funerary objects			Sacred objects and objects of cultural patrimony		
Museum	Number offered for repatriation	Number repatriated	Percent	Number offered for repatriation	Number repatriated	Percent	Number offered for repatriation	Number repatriated	Percent
American Indian	420	390	93	29,400[b]	8,200	28	1,190	1,090	92
Natural History	5,560	3,940	71	182,820	91,360	50	50	50	100
Total	5,980	4,330	72	212,220	99,550	47	1,240	1,140	92

Source: GAO analysis of data provided by the Smithsonian's American Indian and Natural History Museums.

Notes: (1) Because the numbers provided in this table are estimates, we have rounded them to the nearest ten. (2) Totals may not add because of rounding. (3) In addition to repatriating human remains and objects included in this table, the Smithsonian has also returned some Native American items solely because they were illegally acquired by the Smithsonian, or in the case of the American Indian Museum, by the museum's predecessor, the Museum of the American Indian in New York. Specifically, the American Indian Museum has returned about 30 such items, and the Natural History Museum has returned about 19 such items. An item is considered illegally acquired, for example, if the collector did not have the legal right to acquire it.

[a]According to Smithsonian officials, the museums calculate the number of human remains differently. The Natural History Museum calculates the minimum number of individuals. The American Indian Museum currently calculates the minimum number of individuals, but previously used other methods, including counts of individual elements and counts of the number of bone fragments. The minimum number of individuals cannot be estimated for human remains that were repatriated before the counting method was standardized. The total number of human remains includes skeletal material, hair, scalps, and other cultural objects that may contain human remains.

[b]The American Indian Museum Repatriation Manager told us that some of these are lots rather than individual items. A lot generally is a group of human remains or artifacts that are related in some way, but are not individually numbered or identified.

An official with one tribe told us that museum staff provided guidance for submitting the repatriation claim, such as an example of a claim letter to use as a template for his tribe's official request for the human remains. Officials with other tribes told us they appreciated that the museum staffs showed understanding of the tribes' cultural requirements by taking great care to properly handle and transfer the human remains to a burial site. An official from one tribe described how the museum provided special training in addition to coordinating the repatriation activities. In two other instances, tribal officials said some museum staff attended repatriation ceremonies. Officials from several tribes we spoke with also said they had received funding that assisted them in carrying out repatriation activities with the museums.

Items Have Not Been Repatriated for a Variety of Reasons

Many successful repatriations have occurred, but approximately 1,650 human remains, 112,670 funerary objects, and 100 sacred objects offered for repatriation have not been repatriated. Tribes have either not repatriated these items or generally not pursued repatriation because of their lack of resources, cultural beliefs, tribal government issues, the time needed for intertribal coordination, and need for pesticide testing.

- *Lack of resources:* Officials from two tribes told us that, at times, their tribes have lacked the necessary staff to facilitate the return of human remains and funerary objects affiliated to them. Officials from two other tribes said that their tribes did not have an appropriate location to serve as a final resting place for the items offered for return, so they have been unable to proceed with the repatriation process.
- *Cultural beliefs:* In some cases, tribal cultural beliefs prevent repatriation. For example, one tribal official told us that repatriation can have harmful effects on the tribe, including the deceased tribal members associated with the remains or objects. In another instance, one working group of four tribes said that because it has an ongoing dispute with the Natural History Museum, it will not repatriate offered items because the dispute has created a situation where it is spiritually too dangerous for the tribes to deal with the human remains and funerary objects that have been offered for repatriation.

- *Tribal government issues:* In one case, a tribe had a change in leadership that effectively halted any repatriation efforts. In another case, a tribal official told us that the tribe was experiencing political turmoil, and as a result, it was not a good time for the tribe to make decisions, such as deciding to apply for a repatriation grant.
- *Time needed for intertribal coordination:* According to museum officials, in a number of cases, the museums have offered the same items to multiple tribes, and time is needed for those tribes to coordinate and determine the disposition of the items. In another case, human remains were offered to one tribe, but a tribal official explained that the tribe needed time to coordinate with other tribes closely linked to the tribe's ancestral homeland to determine an appropriate burial site.
- *Need for pesticide testing:* The American Indian Museum Repatriation Manager told us that, in the 1990s, the museum offered 96 objects to one tribe as sacred objects but these have not been repatriated because of the possibility of pesticide contamination.[39] The manager said that because the museum lacked the necessary technology to test the objects for pesticides at the time, the tribe placed a moratorium on this repatriation until the museum could provide adequate assurances that the objects were safe to handle.

In these particular situations where the tribes have not yet repatriated items offered to them, the American Indian Museum Repatriation Manager said that the museum will maintain stewardship of the items or pursue other options. For example, in cases where tribes do not pursue repatriation, the museum may ask whether the tribe is amenable to having other tribes repatriate the items. The Natural History Museum's Repatriation Program Manager said that on multiple occasions, his office has attempted to follow up with tribes to determine if they are ready to repatriate human remains and objects offered to them, and plans to wait for these tribes to respond.

The Smithsonian's Repatriation Policies Do Not Discuss How to Handle Culturally Unidentifiable Items

The NMAI Act requires the Smithsonian, upon request, to repatriate culturally affiliated Indian and Native Hawaiian human remains and funerary objects. The act does not discuss how to handle human remains and objects that cannot be culturally affiliated, otherwise referred to as culturally unidentifiable items. Both museums have repatriation policies, but neither policy addresses culturally unidentifiable items. In contrast, a recent NAGPRA regulation that took effect in May 2010 requires, among other things, federal agencies and museums to consult with federally recognized Indian tribes and Native Hawaiian organizations from whose tribal or aboriginal lands the remains were removed before offering to transfer control of the culturally unidentifiable human remains.[40]

We found that both museums could not culturally affiliate some items, but they have treated these items differently. Natural History Museum officials stated that about 340 human remains and about 310 funerary objects are culturally unidentifiable and will be retained by the museum until additional information can be used to determine affiliation. In contrast, the Repatriation Manager at the American Indian Museum stated that the museum cannot always determine the cultural affiliation for human remains and associated funerary objects in its collection; however, through consultation many of these cases have been resolved by tribes stepping forward and serving a custodial role in the respectful treatment and disposition of these items. The manager further stated that the American Indian Museum's philosophy is to ultimately not have any human remains or associated funerary objects within its collection, and the Repatriation Office will continue consulting with tribes and researching viable options regarding the respectful treatment and disposition of all human remains and associated funerary objects within its collection. Furthermore, according to the Chair of the Board of Trustees' Repatriation Committee, the highest priority of the board is the expeditious return of all human remains and associated funerary objects in the museum's collection to culturally affiliated entities regardless of geography or sociopolitical borders.

Museum policies and Smithsonian officials state that, although not required to, the Smithsonian generally looks to NAGPRA and the NAGPRA regulations as a guide to its repatriation process, where appropriate. However, in a May 2010 letter commenting on the NAGPRA regulation on disposition of culturally unidentifiable remains, the Directors of the American Indian and Natural History Museums cited overall disagreement with the regulation, suggesting that it "favors speed and efficiency in making these dispositions at the expense of accuracy." The Directors also described the potential for remains to be transferred to communities other than the communities of origin based on the geographic parameters outlined in the regulation. They noted that such transfers could affect the working relationships that the museums' staff develop with tribe members. Furthermore, they stated that reaching out to tribes to offer remains that were located on their current or historical land is not an ideal approach because tribes submit repatriation requests when they are ready to engage in repatriation activities. Contacting tribes in the manner outlined in the recent NAGPRA regulation, according to the Directors, could push certain tribes into repatriation claims that they may not be capable of facilitating and affect the working relationships that the museums' staff develop with tribe members.

During our review, we spoke to officials from two tribes interested in receiving items the Smithsonian has determined to be culturally unidentifiable. One tribal official believes that all Native Americans are brothers and therefore all Indian human remains should be offered for repatriation to a requesting tribe based on this belief alone. In addition, the American Indian Museum's Board of Trustees told us that one tribe has come forward and offered to take custody of all human remains the museum has determined to be culturally unidentifiable, and rebury them on a special plot on its reservation. In the absence of a Smithsonian policy for these human remains and objects, the Smithsonian's actions in handling culturally unidentifiable items lack transparency for both tribes and policymakers. Tribes don't know how culturally unidentifiable items are to be handled, and they cannot hold the Smithsonian accountable to a particular policy. Officials from both museums, however, suggested that the number of culturally unidentifiable Indian human remains in their collections could decrease as technology improves to provide new evidence of cultural affiliation, at which point the Smithsonian could have the data necessary to determine a cultural affiliation.

Conclusion

The Smithsonian has inventoried, identified, and repatriated thousands of Indian human remains. This represents important progress toward fulfilling one of the nation's important duties to its Native people.

However, at the rate that the Smithsonian is identifying and culturally affiliating the human remains and objects in its collections, it may take decades more for it to complete this process. This process is lengthy in part because the Smithsonian believes it must base every cultural affiliation decision on the best available scientific and historical documentation because of its legal and fiduciary duties. The current process is time consuming and resource intensive, which means that the Smithsonian spends time and resources to make determinations when, in some cases, it may be possible to make quicker determinations.

In addition, the approach that the Smithsonian has taken to establish a Review Committee to monitor and review inventory, identification, and return of Indian human remains and objects does not provide the oversight specified in section 12 of the NMAI Act. The act gives the Review Committee jurisdiction over all Smithsonian museums, and the Smithsonian's reasons for limiting its jurisdiction to the Natural History Museum are unpersuasive. Because the Review Committee is only advisory and does not set policy or make binding decisions, we believe that it could monitor and review the American Indian Museum's repatriation activities without interfering with the sole authority of its Board of Trustees.

Moreover, because the Review Committee is not required to report on Smithsonian repatriation activities annually to Congress, like the NAGPRA Review Committee, Congress continues to lack information on the progress the Smithsonian is making in implementing the NMAI Act. Congress has received little information on the Smithsonian's progress over the last 21 years, and given the amount of additional time the Smithsonian is likely to need to fulfill its repatriation responsibilities, there is no mechanism for Congress to receive regular progress reports in the future.

Also, at the Smithsonian, there is no independent administrative appeals process for tribes that believe the decisions by the Secretary or the Board of Trustees do not satisfy the NMAI Act's requirements. Given that the Administrative Procedures Act does not apply to the Smithsonian, judicial review may not be practical. Currently, the Smithsonian's Board of Regents is the only body whose purview includes oversight of the decisions made by the Secretary of the Smithsonian as well as the American Indian Museum's Board of Trustees. Without an independent appeals process, tribes have no way of holding the Secretary and the Board of Trustees accountable for repatriation decisions.

Finally, the NMAI Act requires the Smithsonian to, upon request, repatriate culturally affiliated Indian and Native Hawaiian human remains and objects, but it is silent on the treatment of items the Smithsonian cannot culturally affiliate. The Smithsonian has not yet clearly articulated its plans for these culturally unidentifiable items. In the absence of such plans, the final disposition of these items is not clear. Tribes or other interested parties thus have no way to hold the Smithsonian accountable for decisions about how or when to retain or repatriate these items.

Matter for Congressional Consideration

Congress may wish to consider ways to expedite the Smithsonian's repatriation process including, but not limited to, directing the Smithsonian to make cultural affiliation determinations as efficiently and effectively as possible.

Recommendations for Executive Action

We are recommending that the Smithsonian Institution's Board of Regents take the following four actions.

- Direct the Secretary of the Smithsonian to expand the Review Committee's jurisdiction to include the American Indian Museum, as required by the NMAI Act, to improve oversight of Smithsonian repatriation activities. With this expanded role for the Review Committee, the Board of Regents and the Secretary should also consider where the most appropriate location for the Review Committee should be within the Smithsonian's organizational structure.
- Through the Secretary, direct the Review Committee to report annually to Congress on the Smithsonian's implementation of its repatriation requirements in the NMAI Act to provide Congress with information on the Smithsonian's repatriation activities.
- Establish an independent administrative appeals process for Indian tribes and Native Hawaiian organizations to appeal decisions to either the Board of Regents or another entity that can make binding decisions for the Smithsonian Institution to provide tribes with an opportunity to appeal cultural affiliation and repatriation decisions made by the Secretary and the Board of Trustees.
- Direct the Secretary and the American Indian Museum's Board of Trustees to develop policies for the Natural History and American Indian Museums for the handling of items in their collections that cannot be culturally affiliated to provide for a clear and transparent repatriation process.

Agency Comments

We provided a copy of this report for review and comment to the Smithsonian Institution. In its written comments, the Smithsonian agreed with the report's findings and recommendations and identified actions that it plans to consider to respond to our recommendations. The Smithsonian's written comments are reprinted in appendix III.

Anu K. Mittal
Director,
Natural Resources and Environment

Appendix I: Objectives, Scope, and Methodology

This appendix details the methods we used to examine the Smithsonian Institution's implementation of the repatriation requirements in the National Museum of the American Indian Act (NMAI Act).[1] We were asked to determine

1. the extent to which the Smithsonian has fulfilled its repatriation requirements and what challenges it faces, if any, in fulfilling its requirements;
2. how the special review committee provisions in the NMAI Act have been implemented and the challenges the committee faces, if any, in fulfilling its requirements; and
3. the number of human remains and objects that have been repatriated and the reasons for those that have not.

For all three objectives, we examined the NMAI Act's implementation at the two Smithsonian museums with collections subject to the act—the American Indian and Natural History Museums.[2] We reviewed the NMAI Act, the Native American Graves Protection and Repatriation Act (NAGPRA) and its implementing regulations, and the museums' repatriation policies. We interviewed officials from the museums' respective repatriation offices and the Smithsonian's Office of General Counsel on the repatriation process. We obtained the Smithsonian's legal views on how it interprets the NMAI Act in writing and also received an additional memorandum regarding its legal views. We reviewed museum data on the total number of human remains and objects the museums have had in their collections through December 31, 2010.

To check the reliability of these data, we interviewed officials and discussed the methodology used in collecting and maintaining these data. Smithsonian officials told us they face a number of challenges in estimating the total number of Indian human remains and objects. For example, the Natural History Museum's Repatriation Office Manager and the American Indian Museum's Curator of Collections Research and Documentation said that their records over time contained different numbers.[3] We also cross-checked the data across multiple source documents and tried to reconcile any differences through discussions with museum staff. Given the challenges with the data, we present the numbers in the report as estimates and we rounded them to the nearest ten. The use of rounding did not materially affect our findings, conclusions, and recommendations because of the large number of human remains and objects. We believe that the data are sufficiently reliable to accurately portray broad trends showing the Smithsonian's progress in implementing the NMAI Act's repatriation requirements.

In addition, during the course of our review, for all three objectives, we traveled to several locations to attend repatriation conferences and visit with tribes.

- *Wisconsin:* We attended the National Association of Tribal Historic Preservation Officers 2010 Annual Conference in Green Bay, Wisconsin, and presented the findings of our July 2010 report on federal agency compliance with NAGPRA.[4] During the conference, we met with several tribes interested in repatriation issues.
- *Oklahoma:* We interviewed the Cheyenne Tribe of Oklahoma and the Choctaw Nation of Oklahoma, who have both repatriated human remains from the Natural History Museum. In addition, we attended a NAGPRA conference held in Oklahoma City that included an address by the Director of the American Indian Museum on repatriation activities at that museum.
- *Alaska:* In Anchorage, Alaska, we interviewed the Director of the Smithsonian Arctic Studies Center, which is housed within the Alaska State Museum. We also interviewed the Director of the Anchorage Museum, who formerly handled repatriation activities for the Kaw Nation of Oklahoma and also served as the Repatriation Manager of the American Indian Museum. We interviewed an official with the

Ukpeagvik Inupiat Corporation who participated in a repatriation with the Natural History Museum. We met with an official from the Native American Rights Fund and one from the Department of the Interior's Bureau of Land Management's Alaska State Office to discuss repatriation issues in Alaska. In Fairbanks, Alaska, we attended the Alaska Federation of Natives 2010 Annual Conference. During the conference, we interviewed members of the Native Village of Crooked Creek to discuss their repatriation experiences.

- *Washington, D.C.:* We attended the NAGPRA at 20 conference commemorating NAGPRA's 20th anniversary. As part of this conference, we attended a panel discussion that included the manager of the American Indian Museum Repatriation Office and the current and former managers of the Natural History Museum Repatriation Office. The panel was focused on the differences between the NMAI Act and NAGPRA.

In addition to the tribes we interviewed during our site visits, we contacted 10 tribes that had completed repatriations with both the American Indian and Natural History Museums and interviewed 2 of them on their experiences with these museums.

To address our first objective, we reviewed museum summaries and inventories to generally determine their contents and if they were prepared within the deadlines in the act. The American Indian Museum prepared inventories in 1993 and 1995 and was able to provide one example of its inventories along with sample cover letters for each year (the American Indian Museum did not prepare separate summaries); the Natural History Museum was able to provide copies of all of its summaries and inventories. We reviewed (1) the American Indian Museum Repatriation Office's progress reports to the museum's Board of Trustees, (2) the Natural History Museum Repatriation Office's progress reports to the Review Committee, and (3) the Review Committee's annual reports to the Secretary of the Smithsonian and meeting minutes.[5] We obtained and reviewed all repatriation claims submitted to the Smithsonian and analyzed all 171 case reports prepared by repatriation staff at both the American Indian and Natural History Museums to collect information about the museums' repatriation activities, including the number of catalog numbers considered in each report. Specifically, where it was available in case reports, we collected information that falls into the following three categories:

- *Repatriation claim:* For case reports that include information about a repatriation claim for one or more items addressed in the report, we recorded the name of the requesting entity or requesting entities, the first date of contact between the Smithsonian and the requesting tribe, the date of the official claim letter, and the date of the report as well as the date of any amendments or addenda to the report. We also recorded descriptive information in the case reports about factors that affected the timeliness with which the Smithsonian addressed the claim.
- *Culturally unidentified remains and funerary objects:* For human remains and funerary objects explicitly identified as culturally unidentified, we recorded the total number of catalog numbers that fall into this category for human remains and funerary objects and, where available, the approximate number of human remains and funerary objects represented by these catalog numbers.
- *Recommendations regarding repatriation:* In cases where the case report includes a recommendation that the Smithsonian repatriate human remains or objects to specific tribes or consult with specific tribes regarding the disposition of remains or objects, we recorded the names of those tribes. We also recorded whether or not the case report recommends that any human remains or objects be retained by the Smithsonian.

Each case report was reviewed by two analysts independently, answers were recorded, results were compared by a third reviewer, and then any differences were reconciled. Using this information, we calculated the length of time from the date of a tribal claim to the date of a case report using available month and year information, where applicable and when such dates were available. In the couple of instances when case reports had no month, we imputed January. We used the date of the official claim letter as the basis for the report-processing times because information on when the Smithsonian actively started working on each claim was not routinely available. As a result, the processing times include the time that the claims were inactive while they were awaiting active consideration. For the Natural History Museum, we used the date that the NMAI Act was originally enacted—November 28, 1989—for claims submitted prior to that time. For the American Indian Museum, we used the date the museum officially took control of its collections—June 1, 1990—for claims submitted prior to that time. We supplemented the case report review by reviewing all claim letters submitted from enactment through

December 2010 to both museums. In the few instances when case reports did not document a claim letter but we found there actually was a claim based on the claim letter review, we added the date to our time frames. We also interviewed officials from the American Indian and Natural History Museums, members of the American Indian Museum's Board of Trustees and the Review Committee, and tribes who have submitted claims for remains or objects held by the Smithsonian to determine any challenges the Smithsonian faces in implementing the NMAI Act's repatriation requirements. For purposes of our analysis, intercoder reliability was measured as the percent agreement between the independent coders and a threshold of 70 percent agreement was used as a basis to assess intercoder reliability. Using percent agreement as a measure of intercoder reliability was appropriate in our case since the majority of the variables coded in this exercise are count variables or nominal variables with multiple possible responses where the likelihood of agreement through mere chance is decreased. Thirteen of the 15 items evaluated achieved an acceptable level of agreement between 74 and 97 percent. For the 2 items in which agreement was less than 70 percent, attempts were made to better understand the pattern of errors and reviewers met to discuss and were able to effectively resolve these inconsistencies. Ultimately, most items, including those 2 items, were not systematically reported on, but rather used for anecdotal purposes.

For our second objective, we examined the Review Committee charter and bylaws. We analyzed the repatriation offices' progress reports and Review Committee annual reports, meeting minutes, and other documents. To document the activities and challenges of the Review Committee, we examined comments made by Review Committee members on repatriation case reports, attended portions of two Review Committee meetings in Washington, D.C., in December 2009 and December 2010,[6] and interviewed 6 of the 7 Review Committee members at each meeting.[7] In addition, we received written comments from the full Review Committee. Because the Board of Trustees has performed oversight of the American Indian Museum's repatriation activities, we interviewed 5 of the 23 board members, 4 of the 8 who make up the board's Repatriation Committee. We met with these 5 members because they were available to meet in between sessions of a board meeting. We also received written comments from the full board. In addition, we reviewed the Administrative Procedures Act and case law interpreting it.

For our third objective, we analyzed museum data as well as specific lists prepared by the museums of the human remains and objects in their collections that were offered for repatriation but never repatriated. We contacted 14 of the 68 tribes or tribal entities to which these human remains and objects were culturally affiliated—8 for the American Indian Museum and 6 for the Natural History Museum—and interviewed 5 of them to determine why the items offered had not been repatriated. The other 9 tribes that we contacted did not respond to our inquiries. We chose tribes in a way to ensure geographic diversity and targeting those with a substantial number of items offered for repatriation. Where items were offered to multiple tribes (of which there were numerous cases), we included at least one of those tribes. We reviewed the repatriation policies of both museums to determine if they covered culturally unidentifiable items. We interviewed Smithsonian officials and both Repatriation Offices to determine if they have a policy for handling culturally unidentifiable items. We interviewed and submitted written questions to both the Review Committee and board about the disposition of culturally unidentifiable items, and we reviewed the Department of the Interior's regulation on culturally unidentifiable items under NAGPRA. We conducted this performance audit from July 2010 to May 2011 in accordance with generally accepted government auditing standards. Those standards require that we plan and perform the audit to obtain sufficient, appropriate evidence to provide a reasonable basis for our findings and conclusions based on our audit objectives. We believe that the evidence obtained provides a reasonable basis for our findings and conclusions based on our audit objectives.

Appendix II: Processing Times for Repatriation Case Reports

This appendix provides (1) overall time frames for completing case reports and factors affecting the time frames and (2) specific details on the processing times for repatriation case reports.

Overall Time Frames for Completing Case Reports and Factors Affecting the Time Frames

The Smithsonian completed 171 case reports from November 28, 1989, through December 31, 2010—at least 126 were completed in response to a claim. The remainder were completed proactively without a claim. For the 41 case reports prepared by the American Indian Museum through 2010 where we identified a claim, we found that it took a median of 1.5 years from the date of an official claim letter to the date a draft case report was submitted to the museum's Board of Trustees for final approval and a repatriation decision.[1] This varied from 3 months to 8.2 years. For the 85 claim-based case reports prepared by the Natural History Museum through 2010, we found that it took a median of 2.8 years from the date of an official claim letter to the date a final case report was approved by the Secretary of the Smithsonian. This varied from 1 month to 18.3 years. We used the date of the official claim letter as the basis for the report-processing times because information on when the Smithsonian actively started working on each claim was not routinely available. As a result, the processing times include the time that the claims were pending while they were awaiting active consideration. We identified examples of claim letters remaining in the queue awaiting active consideration for months and even years before the museums initiated a case report.[2] Case reports prepared by the Smithsonian ranged in length from a 3-page report about the remains of a single individual to a 631-page report that addressed the remains of more than 1,200 individuals and more than 14,400 funerary objects held by the Natural History Museum. On average, case reports prepared by the Natural History Museum considered 33 catalog numbers, while case reports prepared by the American Indian Museum considered 11 catalog numbers. We identified a number of factors that have affected the length of this process, based on information in the case reports. For example, *Repatriation offices were not yet established:* Several claims were submitted to the American Indian and Natural History Museums before they established repatriation offices in November 1993 and September 1991, respectively. *Staffing changes occurred:* We identified examples where staff responsible for preparing the case report left the Smithsonian, resulting in delays to the case report preparation process. *Waiting for tribal response:* In some cases, the museums did not receive needed responses or information from the requesting tribe in a timely manner. For example, in one case a tribe submitted a claim for human remains held by the Natural History Museum and subsequently told the museum that it was opposed to documentation of the remains and asked that the documentation be halted. The museum sought clarification from the tribe on how to proceed, and about 5 months passed before the tribe agreed to allow the museum to continue documentation.

- *Competing claims:* The Natural History Museum gives priority to claims for named individuals. In some cases, a tribe may submit a claim for all human remains and objects potentially affiliated to it, then, later on, a lineal descendant may submit a competing claim. In those cases, the museum may halt its work on the original claim to work on the latter claim.

- *Museum priorities:* Previously, the museums prioritized claims for human remains, resulting in some delays in addressing claims for sacred objects and objects of cultural patrimony. Currently, the Natural History Museum prioritizes claims for named individuals, but otherwise both museums address claims in the order they are received.

In a couple of cases, the museums expedited the case report process and, in other cases, the museum conducted a significant amount of work before receiving an official claim, which may have reduced the length of time needed to complete the report. For example, in one instance, the Natural History Museum agreed to a tribal request to expedite the repatriation process so that the tribe could complete the process at the same time it completed repatriations from the National Park Service. Furthermore, both museums have proactively initiated research and produced case reports about some of the human remains in their collections and, in some instances, later received claims for these human remains. These case reports are included in the time frames provided below.

Specific Details on the Processing Times for Repatriation Case Reports

Table 5 shows the specific details on the processing times for repatriation case reports completed through December 31, 2010.

Table 5. Processing Times for Repatriation Case Reports Completed between November 28, 1989, and December 31, 2010

Date of case report	Date of claim	Elapsed time between claim and case report (in years)	Number of catalog numbers considered
National Museum of the American Indian			
July 1991	Apr. 1991	0.2	2
May 1992	Jan. 1985	1.8	37+[a]
Sept. 1993	Apr. 1993	0.4	87
May 1994[b]	No claim	Not applicable	146+[a]
Jan. 1995	No claim	Not applicable	272

Date of case report	Date of claim	Elapsed time between claim and case report (in years)	Number of catalog numbers considered
Jan. 1995[b]	No claim	Not applicable	36
Feb. 1995	Sept. 1994	0.4	2
Feb. 1995	No claim	Not applicable	1
Feb. 1995	No claim	Not applicable	338
Apr. 1995	No claim	Not applicable	22
Aug. 1995	Sept. 1994	0.9	1
Aug. 1995	No claim	Not applicable	1
Aug. 1995	No claim	Not applicable	3
Sept. 1995	Mar. 1994	1.5	129
Oct. 1995	No claim	Not applicable	1
Oct. 1995	No claim	Not applicable	8
Nov. 1995	No claim	Not applicable	2
Mar. 1996	No claim	Not applicable	1
Mar. 1996	No claim	Not applicable	41
Apr. 1996	No claim	Not applicable	1
Apr. 1996	No claim	Not applicable	1
May 1996	No claim	Not applicable	1
May 1996	No claim	Not applicable	13
June 1996[b]	Feb. 1994	2.3	25
June 1996	No claim	Not applicable	14
May 1997	No claim	Not applicable	1
May 1997	No claim	Not applicable	2
July 1997	Sept. 1995	1.8	3
July 1997	No claim	Not applicable	112
Aug. 1997	Sept. 1995	1.9	97
Sept. 1997	Feb. 1997	0.6	1
Oct. 1997	Oct. 1996	1.0	1
Oct. 1997	No claim	Not applicable	1
Mar. 1998	No claim	Not applicable	1
Apr. 1998[b]	No claim	Not applicable	8
May 1998[b]	Dec. 1994	3.4	451
June 1998	June 1997	1.0	181
Sept. 1998	No claim	Not applicable	3
Oct. 1998	Dec. 1994	3.8	1
Oct. 1998	Nov. 1997	0.9	1
Jan. 1999	Aug. 1997	1.4	2
Jan. 1999	Dec. 1997	1.1	4
Oct. 1999	Aug. 1998	1.2	2
Feb. 2000	Aug. 1998	1.5	1

Table 5. (Continued)

Date of case report	Date of claim	Elapsed time between claim and case report (in years)	Number of catalog numbers considered
Apr. 2000	Sept. 1994	5.6	16
Apr. 2000	July 1999	0.8	22
May 2000	Aug. 1999	0.8	2
May 2000	July 1999	0.8	1
June 2000	Nov. 1999	0.6	14
Oct. 2000	Feb. 1998	2.7	1
Jan. 2002	Oct. 1999	2.3	1
June 2002	July 2001	0.9	1
June 2002	No claim	Not applicable	1
June 2002	No claim	Not applicable	1
June 2002	No claim	Not applicable	5
June 2002	No claim	Not applicable	1
Aug. 2002	No claim	Not applicable	1
Oct. 2002[b]	No claim	Not applicable	4
Aug. 2003	No claim	Not applicable	2
Sept. 2003	June 2003	0.3	1
Aug. 2004	No claim	Not applicable	4
Oct. 2004	Mar. 2000	4.6	19
Nov. 2004	July 2003	1.3	27
May 2005	Oct. 2001	3.6	2
Sept. 2005	Aug. 2004	1.1	3
Dec. 2005	Apr. 2001	4.7	1
Oct. 2006	Mar. 2003	3.6	1
Oct. 2006[b]	Jan. 2004	2.7	43
May 2007	Sept. 2002	4.7	2
June 2007	May 2002	5.1	1
June 2007	No claim	Not applicable	4
May 2009	Feb. 2001	8.2	2
Aug. 2009	Mar. 2004	5.4	9
Aug. 2009	Mar. 2008	1.4	127
June 2010	Jan. 2006	4.4	157
Nov. 2010	No claim	Not applicable	1
National Museum of Natural History			
May 1992	Aug. 1989	2.4	36
July 1992	Aug. 1988	2.6	35
July 1992	Oct. 1989	2.6	56
May 1993	Sept. 1989	3.4	11

Date of case report	Date of claim	Elapsed time between claim and case report (in years)	Number of catalog numbers considered
Aug. 1993	Feb. 1988	3.7	236
Aug. 1993	Aug. 1989	3.7	16
Aug. 1993	Nov. 1989	3.7	19
Sept. 1993	June 1988	3.8	1
Mar. 1994	Jan. 1993	1.2	8
Mar. 1994[b]	July 1993	0.7	1
Apr. 1994	No claim	Not applicable	47
June 1994	No claim	Not applicable	97
Aug. 1994[b]	July 1993	1.1	1
Sept. 1994	Feb. 1994	0.6	7
Oct. 1994	Aug. 1988	4.8	8
Jan. 1995	Aug. 1988	5.1	43
Apr. 1995	Apr. 1990	5.0	13
Apr. 1995	Jan. 1993	2.2	2
June 1995	No claim	Not applicable	32
Aug. 1995	Aug. 1988	5.7	61
Aug. 1995	Mar. 1994	1.4	2
Aug. 1995	No claim	Not applicable	7
Oct. 1995	Aug. 1994	1.2	22
Dec. 1995	July 1993	2.4	13
Feb. 1996	Jan. 1993	3.1	92
Mar. 1996[b]	No claim	Not applicable	102
Apr. 1996[b]	Feb. 1991	5.2	6
Apr. 1996	Sept. 1995	0.6	7
May 1996	July 1992	3.8	29
June 1996	Sept. 1989	6.5	44+[a]
July 1996	Feb. 1996	0.4	339
Aug. 1996	July 1994	2.1	344
Sept. 1996	Nov. 1989	6.8	5
Sept. 1996	Dec. 1993	2.8	440
Sept. 1996[b]	Jan. 1994	2.7	4
Mar. 1997	Aug. 1992	4.6	9
Mar. 1997	June 1995	1.7	18
Apr. 1997	Feb. 1997	0.2	743
Aug. 1997[b]	June 1988	7.7	44
Aug. 1997	Jan. 1993	4.6	38
Dec. 1997	May 1994	3.6	44
July 1998	June 1998	0.1	1
Aug. 1998	Sept. 1986	8.7	2

Table 5. (Continued)

Date of case report	Date of claim	Elapsed time between claim and case report (in years)	Number of catalog numbers considered
Aug. 1998	Nov. 1997	0.7	10+[a]
Mar. 1999	July 1997	1.7	47
Apr. 1999	Sept. 1989	9.3	7
Apr. 1999	No claim	Not applicable	1
May 1999	Aug. 1998	0.7	1
Dec. 1999	Mar. 1999	0.8	69
Jan. 2000	Nov. 1991	8.2	1
Apr. 2000	Nov. 1996	3.4	1
Nov. 2000	Aug. 1996	4.3	1
June 2001	Nov. 1998	2.6	1
Oct. 2001	Oct. 1999	2.0	8
Dec. 2001	Aug. 1989	12.0	7
Apr. 2002	Aug. 1996	5.7	98
July 2002	Feb. 2000	2.4	44
Mar. 2003	Aug. 1994	8.6	18
Mar. 2003	July 2002	0.7	1
Aug. 2003	Jan. 2002	1.6	1
Aug. 2003	Feb. 2002	1.5	1
Mar. 2004	Apr. 1999	4.9	14
Mar. 2004	July 2002	1.7	2
Apr. 2004	No claim	Not applicable	184
May 2004	Feb. 1988	14.4	64
Sept. 2004	Feb. 2004	0.6	3
Feb. 2005	Dec. 1997	7.2	11
Sept. 2005	July 1998	7.2	79
Nov. 2005	June 2004	1.4	4
Dec. 2005	Sept. 1989	16.0	2,054+[a]
Apr. 2006	Oct. 2003	2.5	5
June 2006	Mar. 2004	2.3	7
Oct. 2006	June 2004	2.3	204
Dec. 2006	Aug. 1999	7.3	10
Jan. 2007	Dec. 1998	8.1	1
Feb. 2007	July 1996	10.6	7
Mar. 2007	Oct. 2006	0.4	1
June 2007	July 1996	10.9	3
Sept. 2007	Dec. 2003[c]	3.8	2
Aug. 2008	July 2002	6.1	1

Date of case report	Date of claim	Elapsed time between claim and case report (in years)	Number of catalog numbers considered
Aug. 2008	Jan. 2004	4.6	9
Oct. 2008	Dec. 1998	9.8	33
Oct. 2008	Aug. 2007	1.2	62
Nov. 2008	Nov. 2007	1.0	1
June 2009	Feb. 2008	1.3	133
Sept. 2009	Dec. 2007	1.8	1
Nov. 2009	No claim	Not applicable	2
Apr. 2010[b]	Oct. 1999	10.5	8
Apr. 2010	June 2008	1.8	4
Apr. 2010	No claim	Not applicable	1
Sept. 2010	Jan. 2009	1.7	5
Oct. 2010	No claim	Not applicable	225
Nov. 2010	Aug. 1992	18.3	76
Dec. 2010	Mar. 1993	17.8	23
Dec. 2010	Aug. 2010	0.3	12

Source: GAO analysis of repatriation case reports and claim letters from the Smithsonian's American Indian and Natural History Museums.

Notes: In calculating the processing times for completion of the case reports, we used the date of claim as a starting point, with two exceptions.

First, for the American Indian Museum, we used a starting date of July 1, 1990, for any case reports that had a claim received prior to that date because the museum did not officially take control of its collections until June 21, 1990.

Second, for the Natural History Museum, we used a starting date of December 1, 1989, for any case reports that had a claim received prior to that date because the NMAI Act was enacted on November 28, 1989.

[a]For some case reports, the total number of catalog numbers considered is not clear. In those instances, we provide the minimum number of catalog numbers considered, as indicated by the + symbol.

[b]After completing this report, the museum prepared an amendment or addenda to the report. In some instances, preparing amendments or addenda may involve extensive research, according to officials.

[c]The museum first received a claim in February 2001, but did not receive possession and control of the claimed items until December 2003.

Appendix III: Comments from the Smithsonian Institution

Smithsonian Institution

May 6, 2011

Ms. Anu Mittal
Director
National Resources and Environment
United States Government Accountability Office
441 G Street, NW
Washington, DC 20548

Dear Ms. Mittal:

On behalf of the Smithsonian Institution, I write to express our gratitude to you and the staff of the Government Accountability Office (GAO) for this comprehensive report of the Smithsonian's repatriation activities. With one of the world's largest and most important collections of Native American cultural objects, the Smithsonian Institution has a demonstrated and laudable record of repatriation of Native American human remains and cultural objects. In fact, the Smithsonian was one of the first institutions in the country to return Native American human remains and cultural objects, and engaged in such voluntary returns even prior to the passage of the National Museum of the American Indian (NMAI) Act.

As your report recognizes, the Smithsonian has offered to repatriate close to 6,000 human remains and over 212,000 cultural objects – a record far surpassing any other institution holding objects subject to any repatriation legislation. Similarly, your report gives due credit to the Smithsonian by recognizing that the Institution has gone above and beyond the letter of the law in many respects, including the international repatriations conducted by the National Museum of the American Indian and the repatriations to non-federally recognized tribes (when supported by federally recognized tribes) conducted by the National Museum of Natural History. Such an immense undertaking demonstrates the Smithsonian's commitment to the repatriation process, its responsiveness to the concerns of Native communities, and its respect for the ideals of the legislation.

While the Smithsonian's record is commendable, we recognize that our policies and procedures could be improved and we welcome the GAO's recommendations on how the Smithsonian can better achieve its goals and serve its constituents. I address each recommendation separately below to note the efforts already underway to implement these recommendations.

Expand the jurisdiction of the Review Committee to include the National Museum of the American Indian.

Congress directed that the Board of the Trustees of the National Museum of the American Indian shall have sole authority over the collections of the National Museum of the American Indian. At the same time, Congress created a Review Committee to monitor the repatriation of human remains and funerary objects present in the collections of the Smithsonian. Because of the special delegation of authority given to the Board of Trustees of the National Museum of the American Indian, the Smithsonian has interpreted the jurisdiction of the Review Committee to extend only to the repatriation activities of the National Museum of Natural History. The Smithsonian, nonetheless, agrees with the GAO's recommendation that the advisory nature of the Review Committee could be expanded to include consultation with the National Museum of the American Indian. The Smithsonian has already met with members of the Review Committee to ascertain its view on this recommendation. Additional discussions between Smithsonian senior management, the Board of the Trustees of the National Museum of the American Indian and the Review Committee are necessary to determine how to implement this recommendation, including where the most appropriate location for the Review Committee should be within the Smithsonian's organizational structure.

Direct the Review Committee to report annually to Congress on the Smithsonian's implementation of its repatriation requirements under the NMAI Act.

The NMAI Act does not require any annual reporting to Congress. We recognize, however, that information on the repatriation activities of those entities subject to the Native American Graves Protection and Repatriation Act (NAGPRA) are contained in an annual report submitted by the National NAGPRA Program, and because the Smithsonian is not subject to NAGPRA, information regarding the Smithsonian's repatriation activities is not included in that report. To provide Congress with a complete and robust understanding of the repatriation process on a nationwide level, the Smithsonian, through the Office of the Secretary, will submit, on a voluntary basis, annual reports to Congress. The format and presentation of the report are matters to be discussed internally, but, for consistency and familiarity purposes, the Smithsonian intends to use the National NAGPRA report as a guide and framework for its discussion and report.

Establish an administrative appeal process for Indian tribes and Native Hawaiian organizations to appeal decisions to either the Board of Regents or another entity that can make binding decisions for the Smithsonian Institution.

In over twenty years of repatriation activities at the Smithsonian, only two claims have resulted in a dispute proceeding before our Review Committee. The Review Committee's dispute resolution provisions are seldom tested demonstrating both the infrequency of such disputes and the success of the Smithsonian's repatriation program. The dissatisfaction of the tribal claimants with the lack of an additional appeal process in the most recent dispute proceeding, concluded in 2009, has heightened the Smithsonian's sensitivity to this issue. The Smithsonian will review its dispute resolution procedures, with the understanding that the goal is to ensure that claimants have proper avenues to seek redress from Smithsonian repatriation decisions, including a process for the review of final management determinations. Because such a process is outside the scope of the NMAI Act requirements and represents a departure from the Smithsonian's current practices, the exact nature of the appeal process and its implementation require additional input from a variety of stakeholders, including consultation with the Native community, and continued internal discussion.

Develop policies for the National Museum of Natural History and the National Museum of the American Indian for the handling of items in their collections that cannot be culturally affiliated.

In the House Report accompanying passage of the NMAI Act, Congress stated that the repatriation provisions of the NMAI Act provided a "reasonable method and policy for the repatriation of Indian bones and funerary objects in the possession of the Smithsonian." H. Rep. No. 101-340, at 16 (1989). At the same time, Congress recognized that "many human remains in the collection are of unknown origin and will, therefore, remain in the collection." Id. This evidence of legislative intent is quite different from NAGPRA where the National NAGPRA Review Committee was specifically charged in the legislation with compiling an inventory of culturally unaffiliated human remains and for developing a process for the disposition of such remains. See 25 U.S.C. § 3006(c)(5). Absent a legislative mandate to address these unaffiliated remains, the Smithsonian has focused its efforts on the return of affiliated remains.
Of the entire collection of human remains currently in the possession of the Smithsonian, only a very small percentage are presently considered to be culturally unidentifiable. This low percentage of unaffiliated human remains is a testament to the work of the Smithsonian in employing the best available scientific and historical information to provide cultural affiliations for the majority of these human remains as required by the NMAI Act.

While neither the National Museum of Natural History nor the National Museum of the American Indian has a current policy with respect to culturally unaffiliated human remains, both institutions, in the interests of transparency, are committed to developing policies in this regard. Such policies will give guidance to Native communities and the public as to how the Smithsonian will handle and treat such remains. Discussions have already begun in both museums with respect to the development of such policies. In fact, despite the lack of a definitive policy, the National Museum of the American Indian has already engaged in some voluntary returns of human remains which could not be culturally affiliated with any present day Indian tribe.

Thank you again for your careful consideration of the matters presented in your report. The Smithsonian remains committed to the repatriation process and will continue to refine our practices and procedures in order to comply with both the letter and spirit of the NMAI Act.

Sincerely,

G. Wayne Clough

End Notes

[1] Pub. L. No. 101-185, 103 Stat. 1336-47 (1989), *codified as amended at* 20 U.S.C. §§ 80q to 80q-15. The act defines funerary objects as objects that, as part of a death rite or ceremony of a culture, are intentionally placed with individual human remains, either at the time of burial or later. 20 U.S.C. § 80q-14(4). The act includes the return of Indian human remains and associated Indian funerary objects and the return of Indian funerary objects not associated with Indian human remains. 20 U.S.C. § 80q-9(c),(d).

[2] In this report, we refer to the Repatriation Review Committee simply as the Review Committee.

[3] The Smithsonian was established in 1846 with funds bequeathed to the United States by James Smithson. In accordance with James Smithson's will, the institution was established in Washington, D.C., "for the increase and diffusion of knowledge among men." *See* Act of August 10, 1846, ch. 178, 9 Stat. 102 (1846), *codified as amended at* 20 U.S.C. § 41. To that end, the 1846 act provided for the institution's business to be conducted by a Board of Regents and a Secretary.

[4] Pub. L. No. 101-601, 104 Stat. 3048-58 (1990), *codified at* 25 U.S.C. §§ 3001-3013.

[5] See table 1 for definitions of sacred objects and objects of cultural patrimony. The NMAI Act, as amended, adopted the same definitions for these items as NAGPRA.

[6] GAO, *Native American Graves Protection and Repatriation Act: After Almost 20 Years, Key Federal Agencies Still Have Not Fully Complied with the Act*, GAO-10-768 (Washington, D.C.: July 28, 2010).

[7] National Museum of the American Indian Act Amendments of 1996, Pub. L. No. 104-278, 110 Stat. 3355 (1996). Unless otherwise noted, subsequent references in this report to the NMAI Act are references to the act as amended.

[8] The preponderance of the evidence means more likely than not.

[9] Unless otherwise specified, in this report the term *objects* refers to funerary objects, sacred objects, and objects of cultural patrimony.

[10] Although the American Indian Museum uses the term *Repatriation Department*, for consistency this report uses *Repatriation Office* to refer to the entities at both museums that have primary responsibility for repatriation activities.

[11] In this report, we refer to the Smithsonian's written legal views and the additional memorandum collectively as the Smithsonian's legal views.

[12] At the first meeting, one member had recently passed away, and the Smithsonian was seeking a replacement; at the second meeting, one member was absent for personal reasons.

[13] The NMAI Act cites about 4,000 sets of human remains, but Smithsonian officials said that the correct figure is about 2,600.

[14] Sections 2(6) and 2(7) of the NMAI Act indicate that the Smithsonian had approximately 18,000 human remains. According to the Natural History Museum's Repatriation Program Manager, the 18,000 figure actually refers to the number of museum catalog numbers that include Indian human remains and he was unsure as to the source of the figure as a higher number had been reported to Congress earlier. This figure also did not include the Indian human remains in the American Indian Museum's collection.

[15] The museums refer to the staff who conduct research and prepare case reports differently—the American Indian Museum refers to them as research specialists and the Natural History Museum refers to them as case officers. For consistency, this report refers to both as case officers.

[16] S. Rep. No. 104-350, at 3-4 (1996).

[17] GAO-10-768.

[18] This language appears in section 11, which addresses the inventory, identification, and return of Indian human remains and funerary objects. Section 13 requires the Smithsonian to apply, to the greatest extent practicable, section 11's principles and procedures to the inventory, identification, and return of Native Hawaiian human remains and funerary objects.

19 A *reasonable belief* means whether a third party with no vested interest in any particular outcome would agree with the conclusion reached, according to Smithsonian officials. The *preponderance of the evidence* means more likely than not.

[20] The American Indian Museum's Repatriation Office told us that additional Indian human remains have been identified since the inventories were prepared.

[21] The December 31, 1996, deadline for the completion of the summaries was less than 3 months after the 1996 amendments' enactment on October 9, 1996.

[22] The 16,000 figure differs from the approximately 19,150 figure previously discussed for the Natural History Museum for two reasons. First, the inventories did not include the more than 2,500 human remains that were repatriated between the NMAI's enactment in 1989 and when the inventories were prepared. Second, the 19,150 figure includes catalog numbers as possibly including human remains that have been identified since the inventories were prepared—about 650 catalog numbers through December 2010. The museum listed its uncataloged collections in its inventories, but provided minimal information about these collections.

[23] In its legal views, the Smithsonian stated that its consultation process with Native communities began after the inventories were distributed. However, current American Indian Museum officials and a former Natural History Museum official told us that the museums regularly met with Native communities as inventories were being prepared. For example, Smithsonian staff met with representatives of Native communities to discuss key issues related to the development of the American Indian Museum, including architectural matters, exhibitions, training, and public programs. In stating its legal view that given the statutory definition of inventory one could easily construe the consultation requirement to apply with greater force to the requirement to identify the origins of human remains and funerary objects, the Smithsonian added that it has engaged in lengthy consultations with Native communities and claimants to satisfy the consultation requirement.

[24] The Smithsonian uses the same two-step process to implement the act's summary provision. However, the use of the process for summaries does not raise similar concerns about compliance with the act because the summary was to be (1) followed by consultation with tribal government and Native Hawaiian officials and traditional religious leaders, and (2) based upon available information held by the Smithsonian and describe the scope of the collection, kinds of objects included, reference to geographical location, means and period of acquisition and cultural affiliation, where readily ascertainable.

[25] S. Rep. No. 104-350 (1996).

[26] H. Rep. 101-340(I), at 33 (1989); H. Rep. No. 101-340(II), at 42 (1989).

[27] We consider human remains and objects to be offered for repatriation when the Smithsonian (1) completes its analysis and finds that the remains and objects are subject to repatriation, and (2) notifies all applicable tribes about its findings. The Smithsonian has faced challenges in estimating the total number of catalog numbers as well as human remains and objects in catalog numbers because of shifts over time in counting standards, cataloging issues, and new discoveries of human remains and objects. For this reason, we view the numbers we present as best estimates as indicated by the use of the terms *about* or *approximately*.

[28] The Repatriation Manager at the Natural History Museum estimates that about 2,930 catalog numbers were identified as possibly funerary in that museum's inventories. However, this figure is low because, according to the museum's Repatriation Manager, none of the funerary objects repatriated through December 31, 2010, were identified in the inventories as possibly funerary. The American Indian Museum's Repatriation Manager estimates that about 3,420 catalog numbers have been identified as possibly including funerary objects at that museum since the NMAI Act was enacted.

[29] In some cases, the museums have hired contractors to prepare case reports.

[30] The NMAI Act states that nothing in section 11 of the act—which addresses inventories—shall be interpreted as limiting the authority of the Smithsonian to return or repatriate Indian human remains and funerary objects and that nothing in the summary section may be construed to prevent the Smithsonian from carrying out the repatriation of unassociated funerary objects, sacred objects, or objects of cultural patrimony in a manner that exceeds the requirements of the NMAI Act. In addition, the committee report accompanying the 1989 NMAI Act states that the House Natural Resources Committee wishes to make clear the formal process established by the act "is not meant to be a limitation on any other authority the Smithsonian Institution may have to return human remains and funerary objects." H. Rep. No. 101-340(II), at 26 (1989); H. Rep. No. 101-340(I), at 26 (1989).

[31] S. Rep. No. 101-143, at 1 (1989). This report accompanied an earlier version of the NMAI Act that was not enacted. As reported to the Senate, the bill would have required, among other things, the Smithsonian's Board of Regents to conduct a study and make recommendations as to the final disposition of Indian human remains in the Smithsonian's possession and report to Congress within 3 years on the study and recommendations. S. 978, 101st Cong. (1989) (unenacted).

[32] H. Rep. No. 101-340(II), at 25 (1989); H. Rep. No. 101-340(I), at 15 (1989). The Museum of the American Indian in New York is often referred to as the Heye collection.

[33] This challenge to a repatriation recommendation involved one tribal group's request for an item it had identified as both a sacred object and an object of cultural patrimony. The American Indian Museum case report stated that the item did not meet the statutory definition and therefore should not be repatriated to the group. When the group disagreed with the museum's decision, the board instructed Repatriation Office staff to again consult with the tribal group in person. The staff conducted further consultations and, as a result, ultimately changed the case report to recommend repatriation, and the board reversed its decision and repatriated the object.

[34] H. Rep. 101-340(I), at 33 (1989); H. Rep. No. 101-340(II), at 42 (1989).

[35] The law establishing the Smithsonian required it to report to Congress each session. Act of August 10, 1846, ch. 178, § 3, 9 Stat. 102, 104 (1846), *codified as amended at* 20 U.S.C. § 57. Section 3003 of the Federal Reports Elimination and Sunset Act of 1995 eliminated this reporting requirement to Congress starting 4 years after the date of enactment (fiscal year 1999).

[36] The Under Secretary for Science has been given the authority to approve the reports for the Secretary. Once the Under Secretary for Science approves the report, it is no longer a draft and it is the official finding of the museum.

[37] Pub. L. No. 89-55, 80 Stat. 381, *codified as amended at* 5 U.S.C. §§ 500-559 (1946). *See* Dong v. Smithsonian Institution, 125 F.3d 877, 879 (D. C. Cir. 1997).

[38] Section 14 of the NMAI Act authorizes the Secretary of the Interior to make grants to Indian tribes to assist such tribes in reaching and carrying out agreements with the Smithsonian Board of Regents for the return of Indian human remains and funerary objects under section 11. Smithsonian and Interior officials said that the Secretary of the Interior has not made any grants for this purpose. However, the Smithsonian has allocated funds to assist entities including tribes, tribal organizations, coalitions of tribes, and some international indigenous groups with repatriation activities. Specifically, the Natural History Museum reports that over a 17-year period, between 1994 through 2010, it awarded over 100 grants to outside entities totaling about $400,000, or an average of about 6 grants per year at about $3,800 per grant. The American Indian Museum Repatriation Office provided 4 years of data, covering fiscal years 2007 through 2010, on funding it has used for repatriation activities; it

did not readily have data going further back. During that 4-year period, museum officials reported awarding about $135,350. At the American Indian Museum, these funds can be awarded and used by outside entities or used by museum staff. These funds cover the costs, such as travel and accommodations, associated with (1) tribal consultation visits to view the collection and meet with repatriation office staff and (2) transporting repatriated items back to the tribes.

[39]Pesticides are poisons or toxins used to kill pests by entering the organism through dermal contact (skin), oral ingestion (mouth), or inhalation (nose or mouth). In the past, museums applied pesticide treatments in order to prevent or destroy pests and to preserve the collections. Items considered for repatriation may be tested for several hazardous compounds including arsenic and mercury. Information gathered from pesticide testing and records may help the tribe determine the object's future use and disposition.

[40]75 Fed. Reg. 12378 (Mar. 15, 2010). The final rule also allows museums and federal agencies to transfer control of funerary objects associated with culturally unidentifiable human remains and recommends that such transfers occur if not precluded by federal or state law.

End Notes for Appemdix I

[1] Pub. L. No. 101-185, 103 Stat. 1336-47 (1989), *codified as amended at* 20 U.S.C. §§ 80q1-15.

[2] We contacted one other Smithsonian museum—the National Museum of American History—because we were told that museum might have items subject to the NMAI Act. An official from that museum stated that other than some items returned in the 1980s, prior to the NMAI Act, the museum does not have any items subject to the NMAI Act's repatriation requirements.

[3] In the future, the Natural History Museum Repatriation Manager said that the museum may still catalog more human remains, but that there would be very few.

[4] GAO, *Native American Graves Protection and Repatriation Act: After Almost 20 Years, Key Federal Agencies Still Have Not Fully Complied with the Act*, GAO-10-768 (Washington, D.C.: July 28, 2010).

[5] The annual reports and meeting minutes we examined covered the years 1991 through 2007. For 2008 and 2009, the Review Committee was without a Review Committee coordinator who oversees the transcription of the meeting minutes, which are used to draft the annual reports.

[6] The Smithsonian was originally included as part of our NAGPRA repatriation review. We conducted some preliminary audit work at the Smithsonian from July 2009 through December 2009 before deciding that the Smithsonian's repatriation efforts should be evaluated and reported on separately.

[7] At the first meeting, one member had recently passed away and the Smithsonian was seeking a replacement; at the second meeting one member was absent for personal reasons.

End Notes for Appendix II

[1] There can be several weeks or months between the time when a case report is submitted to the Board of Trustees and when the board approves it, according the American Indian Museum Repatriation Manager.

[2] Both museums had a significant number of pending claims as of December 31, 2010— 25 claims from 10 tribes at the American Indian Museum and 5 claims from 5 tribes at the Natural History Museum. The earliest of these claims dates to 2001. In some cases, pending claims have been addressed in part.

In: Repatriation of Indian Human Remains ISBN: 978-1-62618-258-5
Editor: Laurent B. Daville

Chapter 2

INDIAN ISSUES: KEY FEDERAL AGENCIES' AND THE SMITHSONIAN INSTITUTION'S EFFORTS TO IDENTIFY AND REPATRIATE INDIAN HUMAN REMAINS AND OBJECTS. STATEMENT OF ANU K. MITTAL, DIRECTOR, NATURAL RESOURCES AN ENVIRONMENT, GOVERNMENT ACCOUNTABILITY OFFICE. HEARING ON "FINDING OUR WAY HOME: ACHIEVING THE POLICY GOALS OF NAGPRA"*

WHY GAO DID THIS STUDY

The National Museum of the American Indian Act of 1989 (NMAI Act), as amended in 1996, generally requires the Smithsonian Institution to inventory and identify the origins of its Indian and Native Hawaiian human remains and objects placed with them (funerary objects) and repatriate them to culturally affiliated Indian tribes upon request. According to the Smithsonian, two of its museums—the American Indian and the Natural History

---

* This is an edited, reformatted and augmented version of testimony given on June 16, 2011 before the Senate Committee on Indian Affairs.

Museums—have items that are subject to the NMAI Act. The Native American Graves Protection and Repatriation Act (NAGPRA), enacted in 1990, includes similar requirements for federal agencies and museums. The National NAGPRA office, within the Department of the Interior's National Park Service, facilitates the governmentwide implementation of NAGPRA. Each act requires the establishment of a committee to monitor and review repatriation activities.

GAO's testimony is based on its July 2010 report on NAGPRA implementation (GAO-10-768) and its May 2011 report on Smithsonian repatriation (GAO-11-515).

The testimony focuses on the extent to which key federal agencies have complied with NAGPRA's requirements and the extent to which the Smithsonian has fulfilled its repatriation requirements.

The relevant agencies agreed with the recommendations in both reports and GAO is making no new recommendations at this time.

What GAO Found

GAO found that almost 20 years after NAGPRA was enacted, eight key federal agencies with significant historical collections—Interior's Bureau of Indian Affairs (BIA), Bureau of Land Management, Bureau of Reclamation, U.S. Fish and Wildlife Service and National Park Service; Agriculture's U.S. Forest Service; the U.S. Army Corps of Engineers; and the Tennessee Valley Authority—have not fully complied with the requirements of the act. All of the agencies acknowledged that they still have additional work to do and some have not fully complied with NAGPRA's requirement to publish notices of inventory completion for all of their culturally affiliated human remains and associated funerary objects in the *Federal Register*.

In addition, GAO found two areas of concern with the National NAGPRA office's activities.

First, National NAGPRA had developed a list of Indian tribes for the purposes of carrying out NAGPRA that was inconsistent with BIA's official list of federally recognized tribes and an Interior legal opinion. Second, National NAGPRA did not always screen nominations for NAGPRA Review Committee positions properly.

GAO found that repatriations were generally not tracked or reported governmentwide. However, based on GAO's compilation of federal agencies' repatriation data, through September 30, 2009, federal agencies had repatriated

55 percent of the human remains and 68 percent of the associated funerary objects that had been published in notices of inventory completion.

With regard to the repatriation activities of the Smithsonian, GAO found that since the NMAI Act was enacted more than 21 years ago, the Smithsonian has offered to repatriate about 5,000 human remains, which account for approximately one-third of the total estimated human remains in its collections. GAO found that the Smithsonian has adopted a lengthy and resource-intensive inventory and identification process, which may account for the slow progress of repatriation at the museums.

In some cases, through this process, the Smithsonian did not offer to repatriate human remains and objects because it determined that they could not be culturally affiliated with a tribe. GAO also found that the Smithsonian established a Repatriation Review Committee to monitor and review the repatriation activities of the Natural History Museum but not those of the American Indian Museum.

Although the Smithsonian believes Congress intended to limit the committee's jurisdiction to the Natural History Museum, the statutory language and its legislative history do not support that view. GAO also found that neither the Smithsonian nor the review committee had provided regular information to Congress on the repatriation progress at the Smithsonian, and the Smithsonian had no independent administrative appeals process by which tribes could challenge a repatriation decision in the event of a dispute. Through December 31, 2010, the Smithsonian estimated that, of the items it had offered for repatriation, about three-quarters of the Indian human remains (4,330 out of 5,980) and about half of the funerary objects (99,550 out of 212,220) have been repatriated. In addition, the Smithsonian had not offered to repatriate approximately 340 human remains and 310 funerary objects it could not culturally affiliate, and it does not have a policy on the disposition of these items.

Chairman Akaka, Vice Chairman Barrasso, and Members of the Committee:

I am pleased to be here today to participate in your hearing on federal efforts to repatriate Indian and Native Hawaiian human remains and certain cultural objects.

Many federal agencies have acquired thousands of Indian human remains, funerary objects, sacred objects, and objects of cultural patrimony over hundreds of years. Similarly the Smithsonian Institution has acquired its collections since its establishment in 1846.

These human remains and cultural objects have long been a concern for many Indian tribes and Native Hawaiian communities, who have been determined to provide an appropriate resting place for their ancestors. The National Museum of the American Indian Act (NMAI Act) and the Native American Graves Protection and Repatriation Act (NAGPRA) were enacted, in 1989 and 1990 respectively, in part to address these concerns.[1] The acts generally require the Smithsonian Institution and federal agencies to take certain actions to identify the Indian and Native Hawaiian human remains and cultural objects in their collections, affiliate those remains and objects to a tribe, and upon request repatriate the items to the tribes.[2]

In July 2010, we reported on the implementation of NAGPRA by eight key federal agencies with significant historical collections.[3] These agencies included the Department of the Interior's Bureau of Indian Affairs (BIA), Bureau of Land Management (BLM), Bureau of Reclamation (BOR), U.S. Fish and Wildlife Service (FWS), and National Park Service (NPS); the Department of Agriculture's U.S. Forest Service; the U.S. Army Corps of Engineers (Corps); and the Tennessee Valley Authority (TVA). In May 2011, we reported on the Smithsonian Institution's implementation of the NMAI Act's repatriation requirements as they relate to the collections held by the National Museum of the American Indian and the National Museum of Natural History.[4] Our testimony today summarizes the findings of both of these reports and also includes information on some recent actions that the agencies have taken in response to the recommendations we made in our reports. Both of these reports were performance audits that were conducted in accordance with generally accepted government auditing standards. A detailed description of our scope and methodology is presented in each issued report.

Background

NAGPRA Requirements

NAGPRA requires federal agencies to (1) identify their Native American human remains, funerary objects, sacred objects, and objects of cultural patrimony, (2) try and determine if a cultural affiliation exists with a present day Indian tribe or Native Hawaiian organization, and (3) generally repatriate the culturally affiliated items to the applicable Indian tribe(s) or Native Hawaiian organization(s) under the terms and conditions prescribed in the act. NAGPRA covers five types of Native American cultural items (see table 1).

Table 1. Five Types of Native American Cultural Items Covered by NAGPRA

Item	Definition
Human remains	Physical remains of the body of a person of Native American ancestry. 43 C.F.R. § 10.2(d)(1).
Associated funerary objects	Objects that, as part of the death rite or ceremony of a culture, are reasonably believed to have been placed with individual human remains either at the time of death or later, and both the human remains and associated funerary objects are presently in the possession or control of a federal agency or museum, except that other items exclusively made for burial purposes or to contain human remains shall be considered as associated funerary objects. 25 U.S.C. § 3001(3)(A).
Unassociated funerary objects	Objects that, as part of the death rite or ceremony of a culture, are reasonably believed to have been placed with individual human remains either at the time of death or later, where the remains are not in the possession or control of the federal agency or museum and the objects can be identified by a preponderance of the evidence as related to specific individuals or families or to known human remains or, by a preponderance of the evidence, as having been removed from a specific burial site of an individual culturally affiliated with a particular Indian tribe. 25 U.S.C. § 3001(3)(B).
Sacred objects	Specific ceremonial objects which are needed by traditional Native American religious leaders for the practice of traditional Native American religions by their present day adherents. 25 U.S.C. § 3001(3)(C).
Objects of cultural patrimony	Objects having ongoing historical, traditional, or cultural importance central to the Native American group or culture itself, rather than property owned by an individual Native American, and which, therefore, cannot be alienated, appropriated, or conveyed by any individual regardless of whether or not the individual is a member of the Indian tribe or Native Hawaiian organization and such object shall have been considered inalienable by such Native American group at the time the object was separated from such group. 25 U.S.C. § 3001(3)(D).

Source: NAGPRA and its implementing regulations.

NAGPRA's requirements for federal agencies, museums, and the Secretary of the Interior, particularly the ones most relevant to their historical collections, which were the focus of our July 2010 report, include the following:

- *Compile an inventory and establish cultural affiliation.* Section 5 of NAGPRA requires that each federal agency and museum compile an inventory of any holdings or collections of Native American human remains and associated funerary objects that are in its possession or control. The act requires that the inventories be completed no later than 5 years after its enactment—by November 16, 1995—and in consultation with tribal government officials, Native Hawaiian organization officials, and traditional religious leaders. In the inventory, agencies and museums are required to establish geographic and cultural affiliation to the extent possible based on information in their possession. Cultural affiliation denotes a relationship of shared group identity which can be reasonably traced historically or prehistorically between a present day Indian tribe or Native Hawaiian organization and an identifiable earlier group.[5] Affiliating NAGPRA items with a present day Indian tribe or Native Hawaiian organization is the key to deciding to whom the human remains and objects should be repatriated. If a cultural affiliation can be made, the act requires that the agency or museum notify the affected Indian tribes or Native Hawaiian organizations no later than 6 months after the completion of the inventory. The agency or museum was also required to provide a copy of each notice—known as a notice of inventory completion—to the Secretary of the Interior for publication in the *Federal Register.* The items for which no cultural affiliation can be made are referred to as culturally unidentifiable.[6]
- *Compile a summary of other NAGPRA items.* Section 6 of NAGPRA requires that each federal agency and museum prepare a written summary of any holdings or collections of Native American unassociated funerary objects, sacred objects, or objects of cultural patrimony in its possession or control, based on the available information in their possession. The act requires that the summaries be completed no later than 3 years after its enactment—by November 16, 1993. Preparation of the summaries was to be followed by federal agency consultation with tribal government officials, Native Hawaiian organization officials, and traditional religious leaders. After a valid

claim is received by an agency or museum, and if the other terms and conditions in the act are met, a notice of intent to repatriate must be published in the *Federal Register* before any item identified in a summary can be repatriated.[7]

- *Repatriate culturally affiliated human remains and objects*. Section 7 of NAGPRA and its implementing regulations generally require that, upon the request of an Indian tribe or Native Hawaiian organization, all culturally affiliated NAGPRA items be returned to the applicable Indian tribe or Native Hawaiian organization expeditiously—but no sooner than 30 days after the applicable notice is published in the *Federal Register*—if the terms and conditions prescribed in the act are met.

NAGPRA assigns certain duties to the Secretary of the Interior, which are carried out by the National NAGPRA Program Office (National NAGPRA) within NPS. In accordance with NAGPRA's implementing regulations, National NAGPRA has developed a list of Indian tribes and Native Hawaiian organizations for the purposes of carrying out the act. The list is comprised of federally recognized tribes, Native Hawaiian organizations, and, at various points in the last 20 years, corporations established pursuant to the Alaska Native Claims Settlement Act (ANCSA).[8] Since the enactment of two recognition laws in 1994,[9] BIA has regularly published a comprehensive list of recognized tribes—commonly referred to as the list of federally recognized tribes—that federal agencies are supposed to use to identify federally recognized tribes. The recognition of Alaska Native entities eligible for the special programs and services provided by the United States to Indians because of their status as Indians has been controversial. Since a 1993 legal opinion by the Solicitor of the Department of the Interior,[10] BIA's list of federally recognized tribes has not included any ANCSA group, regional, urban, and village corporations.

Finally, NAGPRA requires the establishment of a committee to monitor and review the implementation of inventory, identification and repatriation activities under the act. Among other things, the Review Committee is responsible for, upon request, reviewing and making findings related to the identity or cultural affiliation of cultural items or the return of such items and facilitating the resolution of any disputes among Indian tribes, Native Hawaiian organizations, and federal agencies or museum relating to the return of such items. We refer to these findings, recommendations and facilitation of disputes that do not involve culturally unidentifiable human remains simply as disputes; the Review Committee also makes recommendations regarding the disposition of culturally unidentifiable human remains. The NAGPRA Review Committee was established in 1991.

NMAI Act Requirements

The NMAI Act sections 11 and 13 generally require the Smithsonian to (1) inventory the Indian and Native Hawaiian human remains and funerary objects in its possession or control, (2) identify the origins of the Indian and Native Hawaiian human remains and funerary objects using the "best available scientific and historical documentation," and (3) upon request repatriate them to lineal descendants or culturally affiliated Indian tribes and Native Hawaiian organizations. As originally written, the act did not set a deadline for the completion of these tasks, but amendments in 1996 added a June 1, 1998, deadline for the completion of inventories.[11] The 1996 amendments also require the Smithsonian to prepare summaries for unassociated funerary objects, sacred objects, and objects of cultural patrimony by December 31, 1996.

The NMAI Act uses the same definitions as NAGPRA for unassociated funerary objects, sacred objects, and objects of cultural patrimony,[12] but the NMAI Act does not define human remains and it does not use the term associated funerary objects. Instead, the NMAI Act requires Indian funerary objects—which it defines as objects that, as part of the death rite or ceremony of a culture, are intentionally placed with individual human remains, either at the time of death or later—to be included in inventories and unassociated funerary objects to be included in summaries.

The Smithsonian has identified two museums that hold collections subject to the NMAI Act: the National Museum of the American Indian and the National Museum of Natural History. Final repatriation decisions for the American Indian Museum are made by its Board of Trustees and the Secretary of the Smithsonian has delegated responsibility for making final repatriation decisions for the Natural History Museum to the Smithsonian's Under Secretary for Science.

According to Smithsonian officials, when new collections are acquired, the Smithsonian assigns an identification number—referred to as a catalog number—to each item or set of items at the time of the acquisition or, in some cases, many years later. A single catalog number may include one or more human bones, bone fragments, or objects, and it may include the remains of one or more individuals. All of this information is stored in the museums' electronic catalog system, which is partly based on historical paper card catalogs. Generally, each catalog number in the electronic catalog system includes basic information on the item or set of items, such as a brief description of the item, where the item was collected, and when it was taken into the museum's collection. Since the NMAI Act was enacted, the Smithsonian has identified approximately 19,780 catalog numbers that potentially include Indian human remains (about 19,150 within the Natural History Museum collections and about 630 within the American Indian Museum collections). Finally, like NAGPRA, the NMAI Act requires the establishment of a committee to monitor and review the inventory, identification, and return of Indian human remains and cultural objects. The Smithsonian Review Committee was established in 1990 for this purpose.[13]

After Almost 20 Years, Key Federal Agencies Still Have Not Fully Complied with NAGPRA

As we reported in July 2010, federal agencies have not yet fully complied with all of the requirements of NAGPRA. Specifically, we found that while the eight key federal agencies generally prepared their summaries and inventories on time, they had not fully complied with other NAGPRA requirements. In addition, we found that while the NAGPRA Review Committee had conducted a number of activities to fulfill its responsibilities under NAGPRA, its recommendations have had mixed success. Furthermore, while National NAGPRA has taken several actions to implement the act's requirements, in some cases it has not effectively carried out its responsibilities. Finally, although the key agencies have repatriated many NAGPRA items, repatriation activity has generally not been tracked or reported governmentwide.

Key Federal Agencies Have Not Fully Complied with NAGPRA for Their Historical Collections

The eight key federal agencies we reviewed in our July 2010 report generally prepared their summaries and inventories by the statutory deadlines, but the amount of work put into identifying their NAGPRA items and the quality of the documents prepared varied widely. Of these eight agencies, the Corps, the Forest Service, and NPS did the most extensive work to identify their NAGPRA items, and therefore they had the highest confidence level that they had identified all of them and included them in the summaries and inventories that they prepared. In contrast, relative to these agencies, we determined that BLM, BOR, and FWS were moderately successful in identifying their NAGPRA items and including them in their summaries and inventories, and BIA and TVA had done the least amount of work. As a result, these five agencies had less confidence that they had identified all of their NAGPRA items and included them in summaries and inventories. In addition, not all of the culturally affiliated human remains and associated funerary objects had been published in a *Federal Register* notice as required. For example, at the time of our report, BOR had culturally affiliated 76 human remains but had not published them in a *Federal Register* notice. All of the agencies acknowledged that they still have additional work to do and some had not fully complied with NAGPRA's requirement to publish notices of inventory completion for all of their culturally affiliated human remains and associated funerary objects in the *Federal Register*.

As a result of these findings, we recommended the agencies develop and provide to Congress a needs assessment listing specific actions, resources, and time needed to complete the inventories and summaries required by NAGPRA. We further recommended that the agencies develop a timetable for the expeditious publication in the *Federal Register* of notices of inventory completion for all remaining Native American human remains and associated funerary objects that have been culturally affiliated in inventories. The Departments of Agriculture and the Interior and TVA agreed with our recommendations. For example, Interior stated that this effort is under way in most of its bureaus and that it is committed to completing the process. It added that one of the greatest challenges to completing summaries and inventories of all NAGPRA items is locating collections and acquiring information from the facilities where the collections are stored.

The NAGPRA Review Committee Has Monitored Compliance with NAGPRA Implementation and Made Recommendations with Mixed Success

We found that the NAGPRA Review Committee, to fulfill its responsibilities under NAGPRA, had monitored federal agency and museum compliance, made recommendations to improve implementation, and assisted the Secretary in the development of regulations. As we reported, the committee's recommendations to facilitate the resolution of disposition requests involving culturally unidentifiable human remains have generally been implemented (52 of 61 requests has been fully implemented). In disposition requests, parties generally agreed in advance to their preferred manner of disposition and, in accordance with the regulations, came to the committee to complete the process and obtain a final recommendation from the Secretary. In contrast to the amicable nature of disposition requests, disputes are generally contentious, and we found that the NAGPRA Review Committee's recommendations have had a low implementation rate. Specifically, of the 12 disputes that we reviewed, the committee's recommendations were fully implemented for 1 dispute, partially implemented in 3 others, not implemented for 5, and the status of 3 cases is unknown.

Moreover, we found that some actions recommended by the committee exceeded NAGPRA's scope, such as recommending repatriation of culturally unidentifiable human remains to non-federally recognized Indian groups. However, we found that the committee, National NAGPRA, and Interior officials had since taken steps to address this issue.

National NAGPRA Has, in Some Cases, Not Effectively Carried out Its Responsibilities

We reported that National NAGPRA had taken several actions to help the Secretary carry out responsibilities under NAGPRA. For example, National NAGPRA had published federal agency and museum notices in the Federal Register; increasing this number in recent years, while reducing the backlog of notices awaiting publication. Furthermore, it had administered a NAGPRA grants program that from fiscal years 1994 through 2009 resulted in 628 grants awarded to Indian tribes, Native Hawaiian organizations, and museums totaling $33 million. It had also administered the nomination process for NAGPRA Review Committee members.

Overall, we found that most of the actions performed by National NAGPRA were consistent with the act, but we identified concerns with a few actions. Specifically, National NAGPRA had developed a list of Indian tribes for the purposes of carrying out NAGPRA, but at various points in the last 20 years the list had not been consistent with BIA's policy or an Interior Solicitor legal opinion analyzing the status of Alaska Native villages as Indian tribes.

As a result, we recommended that National NAGPRA, in conjunction with Interior's Office of the Solicitor, reassess whether ANCSA corporations should be considered as eligible entities for the purposes of carrying out NAGPRA. Interior agreed with this recommendation and, after our report was issued, Interior's Office of the Solicitor issued a memorandum in March 2011 stating that NAGPRA clearly does not include Alaska regional and village corporations within its definition of Indian tribes and that the legislative history confirms that this was an intentional omission on the part of Congress. The memorandum also states that while the National NAGPRA Program's list of Indian tribes for purposes of NAGPRA must not include ANCSA regional and village corporations, National NAGPRA is currently bound by its regulatory definition of Indian tribe that contradicts the statutory definition by including ANCSA corporations. Because of this, the Solicitor suggests that the regulatory definition be changed as soon as feasible, followed by a corresponding change in the list.

We also found that National NAGPRA did not always properly screen nominations for the NAGPRA Review Committee and, in 2004, 2005, and 2006, inappropriately recruited nominees for the committee, in one case recommending the nominee to the Secretary for appointment. As a result, we recommended that the Secretary of the Interior direct National NAGPRA to strictly adhere to the nomination process prescribed in the act and, working with Interior's Office of the Solicitor as appropriate, ensure that all NAGPRA Review Committee nominations are properly screened to confirm that the nominees and nominating entities meet statutory requirements. Interior agreed with this recommendation, stating that the committee nomination procedures were revised in 2008 to ensure full transparency and that it will ask the Solicitor's Office to review these procedures.

Repatriations Are Not Tracked or Reported Governmentwide, but According to Data Collected by GAO, Many NAGPRA Items Have Been Repatriated

In July 2010 we reported that while agencies are required to permanently document their repatriation activities, they are not required to compile and report that information to anyone. Of the federal agencies that have published notices of inventory completion, we determined that only three have tracked and compiled agencywide data on their repatriations—the Forest Service, NPS, and the Corps. These three agencies, however, along with other federal agencies that have published notices of inventory completion, do not regularly report comprehensive data on their repatriations to National NAGPRA, the NAGPRA Review Committee, or Congress. Through data provided by these three agencies, along with our survey of other federal agencies, we found that federal agencies had repatriated a total of 55 percent of human remains and 68 percent of associated funerary objects that had been published in notices of inventory completion as of September 30, 2009. Agency officials identified several reasons why some human remains and associated funerary objects had not been repatriated, including the lack of repatriation requests from culturally affiliated entities, repatriation requests from disputing parties, a lack of reburial sites, and a lack of financial resources to complete the repatriation. Federal agencies had also published 78 notices of intent to repatriate that covered 34,234 unassociated funerary objects, sacred objects, or objects of cultural patrimony.

Due to a lack of governmentwide reporting, we recommended the Secretaries of Agriculture, Defense, and the Interior and the Chief Executive Officer of the Tennessee Valley Authority direct their cultural resource management programs to report their repatriation data to National NAGPRA on a regular basis, but no less than annually, for each notice of inventory completion they have or will publish. Furthermore, we recommended that National NAGPRA make this information readily available to Indian tribes and Native Hawaiian organizations and that the NAGPRA Review Committee publish the information in its annual report to Congress. The Departments of Agriculture and the Interior and TVA agreed with this recommendation, and Interior stated that its agencies will work toward completing an annual report beginning in 2011.

The Smithsonian Still Has Much Work to Do to Identify and Repatriate Indian Human Remains and Objects

In our May 2011 report we found that the Smithsonian Institution still had much work remaining with regard to the repatriation activities required by the NMAI Act. Specifically, we found that while the American Indian and Natural History Museums generally prepared summaries and inventories within the statutory deadlines the process that the Smithsonian relies on is lengthy and resource intensive. Consequently, after more than 2 decades, the museums have offered to repatriate the Indian human remains in only about one-third of the catalog numbers identified as possibly including such remains since the act was passed. In addition, we found that the Smithsonian established a Review Committee to meet the statutory requirements, but limited its oversight of repatriation activities. Finally, we found that while the Smithsonian has repatriated most of the human remains and many of the objects that it has offered for repatriation, it has no policy on how to address items that are culturally unidentifiable.

Since 1989, the Smithsonian Has Prepared Required Summaries and Inventories and Has Offered to Repatriate about One-Third of Its Indian Human Remains

We found that while the American Indian and Natural History Museums had generally prepared summaries and inventories within the deadlines established in the NMAI Act, their inventories and the process they used to prepare them have raised questions about their compliance with some of the act's statutory requirements. The first question was the extent to which the museums prepared their inventories in consultation and cooperation with traditional Indian religious leaders and government officials of Indian tribes, as required by the NMAI Act. Section 11 of the act directs the Secretary of the Smithsonian, in consultation and cooperation with traditional Indian religious leaders and government officials of Indian tribes, to inventory the Indian human remains and funerary objects in the possession or control of the Smithsonian and, using the best available scientific and historical documentation, identify the origins of such remains and objects. However, the Smithsonian generally began the consultation process with Indian tribes after the inventories from both museums were distributed. The Smithsonian maintains that it is in full compliance with the statutory requirements for preparing inventories and that section 11 does not require that consultation occur prior to the inventory being completed.

The second question is the extent to which the Natural History Museum's inventories—which were finalized after the 1996 amendments—identified geographic and cultural affiliations to the extent practicable based on available information held by the Smithsonian, as required by the amendments. The museum's inventories generally identified geographic and cultural affiliations only where such information was readily available in the museum's electronic catalog. However, the Smithsonian states that it does not interpret section 11 as necessarily requiring that the inventory and identification process to occur simultaneously, and therefore it has adopted a two-step process to fulfill section 11's requirements. The legislative history of the 1996 amendments provides little clear guidance concerning the meaning of section 11. However, we also found that the two-step process that the Smithsonian has adopted is a lengthy and resource-intensive one and that, at the pace that the Smithsonian is applying this process, it will take several more decades to complete this effort.

As a result of the identification and inventory process the Smithsonian is using, since the passage of the NMAI Act in 1989 through December 2010, the Smithsonian estimates that it has offered to repatriate approximately one-third of the estimated 19,780 catalog numbers identified as possibly including Indian human remains. The American Indian Museum had offered to repatriate human remains in about 40 percent (about 250) of its estimated 630 catalog numbers. The Natural History Museum had offered to repatriate human remains in about 25 percent (about 5,040) of its estimated 19,150 catalog numbers containing Indian human remains. In some cases, through this process, the Smithsonian did not offer to repatriate human remains and objects because it determined that they could not be culturally affiliated with a tribe. The congressional committee reports accompanying the 1989 act indicate that the Smithsonian estimated that the identification and inventory of Indian human remains as well as notification of affected tribes and return of the remains and funerary objects would take 5 years.[14] However, more than 21 years later, these efforts are still under way. In light of this slow progress, we suggested that Congress may wish to consider ways to expedite the Smithsonian's repatriation process including, but not limited to, directing the Smithsonian to make cultural affiliation determinations as efficiently and effectively as possible.

The Smithsonian Review Committee's Oversight and Reporting Are Limited

In May 2011, we reported that the Smithsonian Review Committee had conducted numerous activities to implement the special committee provisions in the NMAI Act, but its oversight and reporting activities have been limited. For example, we found that contrary to the NMAI Act, the committee does not monitor and review the American Indian Museum's inventory, identification, and repatriation activities, although it does monitor and review the Natural History Museum's inventory, identification, and repatriation activities.

Although the law does not limit the applicability of the Smithsonian Review Committee to the Natural History Museum, the Secretary established a committee to meet this requirement in 1990 that oversees only the Natural History Museum's repatriation activities and is housed within that museum. Although the Smithsonian believes Congress intended to limit the committee's jurisdiction to the Natural History Museum, the statutory language and its legislative history do not support that view. The Smithsonian provided several reasons to support this contention but, as we reported in May 2011, these reasons are unpersuasive. Therefore, we recommended that the Smithsonian's Board of Regents direct the Secretary of the Smithsonian to expand the Smithsonian Review Committee's jurisdiction to include the American Indian Museum, as required by the NMAI Act, to improve oversight of Smithsonian repatriation activities. With this expanded role for the committee, we further recommended that the Board of Regents and the Secretary should consider where the most appropriate location for the Smithsonian Review Committee should be within the Smithsonian's organizational structure. The Smithsonian agreed with this recommendation, stating that the advisory nature of the committee could be expanded to include consultation with the American Indian Museum.

In our May 2011 report, we also found that neither the Smithsonian nor the Smithsonian Review Committee submits reports to Congress on the progress of repatriation activities at the Smithsonian. Although section 12 of the NMAI Act requires the Secretary, at the conclusion of the work of the committee, to so certify by report to Congress, there is no annual reporting requirement similar to the one required for the NAGPRA Review Committee. As we stated earlier, in 1989, it was estimated that the Smithsonian Review Committee would conclude its work in about 5 years and cease to exist at the end of fiscal year 1995. Yet the committee's monitoring and review of repatriation activities at the Natural History Museum has been ongoing since the committee was established in 1990. As a result, we recommended that the Board of Regents, through the Secretary, direct the Smithsonian Review Committee to report annually to Congress on the Smithsonian's implementation of its repatriation requirements in the NMAI Act. The Smithsonian agreed with this recommendation, stating that it will submit, on a voluntary basis, annual reports to Congress. The Smithsonian further stated that although the format and presentation are matters to be discussed internally, it intends to use the National NAGPRA report as a guide and framework for its discussion and report.

Finally, during our review of the Smithsonian Review Committee activities we determined that no independent administrative appeals process exists to challenge the Smithsonian's cultural affiliation and repatriation decisions, in the event of a dispute. As a result, we recommended that the Board of Regents establish an independent administrative appeals process for Indian tribes and Native Hawaiian organizations to appeal decisions to either the Board of Regents or another entity that can make binding decisions for the Smithsonian Institution to provide tribes with an opportunity to appeal cultural affiliation and repatriation decisions made by the Secretary and the American Indian Museum's Board of Trustees. The Smithsonian agreed with this recommendation, stating that it will review its dispute resolution procedures, with the understanding that the goal is to ensure that claimants have proper avenues to seek redress from Smithsonian repatriation decisions, including a process for the review of final management determinations.

Most Human Remains and Many Objects Offered for Repatriation Have Been Repatriated, but the Smithsonian Has No Policy on Culturally Unidentifiable Items

In May 2011 we reported that the Smithsonian estimates that, of the items it has offered for repatriation, as of December 31, 2010, it has repatriated about three-quarters (4,330 out of 5,980) of the Indian human remains, about half (99,550 out of 212,220) of the funerary objects, and nearly all (1,140 out of 1,240) sacred objects and objects of cultural patrimony. Some items have not been repatriated for a variety of reasons, including tribes' lack of resources, cultural beliefs, and tribal government issues.

In addition, we found that, in the inventory and identification process, the Smithsonian determined that some human remains and funerary objects were culturally unidentifiable. In some of those cases it did not offer to repatriate the items and it does not have a policy on how to undertake the ultimate disposition of such items. Specifically, our report found that according to Natural History Museum officials about 340 human remains and about 310 funerary objects are culturally unidentifiable. The NMAI Act does not discuss how the Smithsonian should handle human remains and objects that cannot be culturally affiliated, and neither museum's repatriation policies describe how they will handle such items. In contrast, a recent NAGPRA regulation that took effect in May 2010 requires, among other things, federal agencies and museums to consult with federally recognized Indian tribes and Native

Hawaiian organizations from whose tribal or aboriginal lands the remains were removed before offering to transfer control of the culturally unidentifiable human remains.[15] Although Smithsonian officials told us that the Smithsonian generally looks to NAGPRA and the NAGPRA regulations as a guide to its repatriation process, where appropriate, in a May 2010 letter commenting on the NAGPRA regulation on disposition of culturally unidentifiable remains, the Directors of the American Indian and Natural History Museums cited overall disagreement with the regulation, suggesting that it "favors speed and efficiency in making these dispositions at the expense of accuracy." Nevertheless, in our May 2011 report, we recommended that the Smithsonian's Board of Regents direct the Secretary and the American Indian Museum's Board of Trustees to develop policies for the Natural History and American Indian Museums for the handling of items in their collections that cannot be culturally affiliated to provide for a clear and transparent repatriation process. The Smithsonian agreed with this recommendation, stating that both the American Indian and Natural History Museums, in the interests of transparency, are committed to developing policies in this regard and that such policies will give guidance to Native communities and the public as to how the Smithsonian will handle and treat such remains.

In conclusion, Chairman Akaka, Vice Chairman Barrasso, and Members of the Committee, our two studies clearly show that while federal agencies and the Smithsonian have made progress in identifying and repatriating thousands of Indian human remains and objects, after 2 decades of effort, much work still remains to be done to address the goals of both NAGPRA and the NMAI Act. In this context, we believe that it is imperative for the agencies to implement our recommendations to ensure that the requirements of both acts are met and that the processes they employ to fulfill the requirements are both efficient and effective.

This concludes my prepared statement. I would be pleased to answer any questions that you may have at this time.

End Notes

[1] National Museum of the American Indian Act, Pub. L. No. 101-185, 103 Stat. 1336-47 (1989), *codified as amended at* 20 U.S.C. §§ 80q to 80q-15. Native American Graves Protection and Repatriation Act, Pub. L. No. 101-601, 104 Stat. 3048-58 (1990), *codified at* 25 U.S.C. §§ 3001-3013. NAGPRA uses the term *Native American*, while the NMAI Act uses the term *Indian*. In this statement's discussion of each law, we will use the term used in that

law. In the rare instances where we refer to the items covered by both acts collectively, we will simply use the term *Indian*.

[2] NAGPRA defines a federal agency as any department, agency, or instrumentality of the United States, except the Smithsonian Institution. NAGPRA also applies to museums and defines them as any institution or state or local government agency, including any institution of higher learning, that receives federal funds and has possession of, or control over, Native American cultural items, except the Smithsonian Institution. In addition, unless otherwise specified, in this statement the terms objects and cultural objects refer to funerary objects, sacred objects, and objects of cultural patrimony.

[3] GAO, *Native American Graves Protection and Repatriation Act: After Almost 20 Years, Key Federal Agencies Still Have Not Fully Complied with the Act*, GAO-10-768 (Washington, D.C.: July 28, 2010). NAGPRA has a separate provision for Native American items newly excavated or discovered on federal or tribal lands after the date of enactment, referred to as new or inadvertent discoveries and intentional excavations. New or inadvertent discoveries and intentional excavations are covered in section 3 of the act (25 U.S.C. § 3002) and the identification and repatriation of NAGPRA items within collections that existed on or before the date of enactment, referred to as historical collections, are covered in sections 5, 6, and 7 (25 U.S.C. §§ 3003-3005). In accordance with NAGPRA's implementing regulations, section 5, 6, and 7 also apply to collections federal agencies and museums acquire, from sources other than federal or tribal land, after NAGPRA's enactment. Our July 2010 report focused on federal agencies' historical collections.

[4] GAO, *Smithsonian Institution: Much Work Still Needed to Identify and Repatriate Indian Human Remains and Objects*, GAO-11-515 (Washington, D.C.: May 25, 2011).

[5] 25 U.S.C. § 3001(2).

[6] NAGPRA's implementing regulations direct federal agencies and museums to retain possession of culturally unidentifiable human remains pending promulgation of 43 C.F.R. § 10.11 (the regulation to govern the disposition of culturally unidentifiable human remains) unless legally required to do otherwise, or recommended to do otherwise by the Secretary of the Interior. Recommendations regarding the disposition of culturally unidentifiable human remains may be requested prior to final promulgation of 43 C.F.R. § 10.11. 43 C.F.R. § 10.9(e)(6). The regulation to govern the disposition of culturally unidentifiable human remains, 43 C.F.R. § 10.11, was promulgated on March 15, 2010, and became effective on May 14, 2010. 75 Fed. Reg. 12378 (Mar. 15, 2010).

[7] 43 C.F.R. § 10.8(f).

[8] Pub. L. No. 92-203, 85 Stat. 688 (1971), *codified as amended at* 43 U.S.C. §§ 1601-1629h.

[9] The Federally Recognized Indian Tribe List Act of 1994, Pub. L. No. 103-454, Title I (1994); Tlingit and Haida Status Clarification Act, Pub. L. No. 103-454, Title II (1994).

[10] Op. Sol. Int. M-36975 (Jan. 11, 1993).

[11] National Museum of the American Indian Act Amendments of 1996, Pub. L. No. 104-278, 110 Stat. 3355 (1996). Unless noted otherwise, subsequent references in this report to the NMAI Act are references to the act as amended.

[12] 20 U.S.C. § 80q-9a(a).

[13] The Smithsonian refers to its Review Committee as the Repatriation Review Committee. In this statement, we will refer to it as the Smithsonian Review Committee to clearly differentiate it from the NAGPRA Review Committee.

[14] H. Rep. No. 101-340(I), at 33 (1989); H. Rep. No. 101-340(II), at 42 (1989).

[15] 75 Fed. Reg. 12378 (Mar. 15, 2010). The final rule also allows museums and federal agencies to transfer control of funerary objects associated with culturally unidentifiable human remains and recommends that such transfers occur if not precluded by federal or state law.

In: Repatriation of Indian Human Remains ISBN: 978-1-62618-258-5
Editor: Laurent B. Daville

Chapter 3

TESTIMONY OF KEVIN GOVER, DIRECTOR, NATIONAL MUSEUM OF THE AMERICAN INDIAN. HEARING ON "FINDING OUR WAY HOME: ACHIEVING THE POLICY GOALS OF NAGPRA"*

Mr. Chairman and members of the Committee, I am Kevin Gover, director of the Smithsonian Institution's National Museum of the American Indian. I am here today on behalf of the Smithsonian Institution to share with you our record in implementing the repatriation provisions of the National Museum of the American Indian Act.

The Smithsonian Institution is home to two museums that possess collections of Native American materials. The National Museum of Natural History (NMNH) collections include collections of archaeological, ethnological, and physical anthropological materials. The National Museum of the American Indian (NMAI) holds archaeological and ethnological collections. The NMNH opened its doors in 1910. The NMAI was established by Congress in 1989 in the National Museum of the American Indian Act, and its Mall museum opened its doors in 2004. Both Smithsonian museums possess vast collections compiled largely in the 19th and early 20th centuries.

Collecting practices in those times were very different from our current collecting practices. Those old practices sometimes disregarded the values and

---

* This is an edited, reformatted and augmented version of testimony given on June 16, 2011 before the Senate Committee on Indian Affairs.

sensibilities of the Native communities from which the materials originated. As a result, both collections contain materials that properly should reside in the Native communities from which they came. When Congress passed the NMAI Act in 1989, it directed the Smithsonian to undertake the repatriation of human remains and funerary objects. In 1996, Congress amended the NMAI Act to add sacred objects and objects of cultural patrimony to the materials to be repatriated when requested by a tribe or eligible individual.

The Smithsonian has assumed the responsibility with considerable energy. In just over twenty years, the Smithsonian has offered for repatriation nearly 6,000 human remains, over 212,000 funerary objects, and over 1200 sacred objects and objects of cultural patrimony. For a variety of reasons ranging from the cultural to the practical, not all of these offers were accepted. Because of the vastness of the collections of the two museums, moreover, many remains and objects that might be repatriated are still in the collections despite the aggressive repatriation programs of the two museums.

As you know, the General Accountability Office (GAO) has completed a review of the Smithsonian's repatriation activities. We appreciate the GAO's work and the manner in which it was conducted, and recognize that the report raises worthy issues for the consideration of this Committee and the Smithsonian leadership.

Perhaps the most important issue presented by the GAO report involves the tension between the statutory objective of promptly returning eligible materials to requesting tribes and individuals on the one hand, and the statutory objective of returning eligible materials to the *correct* claimants on the other. As noted in the report, the NMAI Act requires the Smithsonian to consider the best available historical and scientific documentation in making its repatriation decisions. This requirement imposes a higher burden of proof on Smithsonian museums than is contemplated under the Native American Graves Protection and Repatriation Act (NAGPRA). It is a requirement both burdensome and necessary. The Smithsonian is committed to the advancement and diffusion of knowledge. Knowledge is the product of thorough research and analysis. Such scholarship produces conclusions that are as accurate as practicable. In the context of our repatriation activities, this means that our decisions should correctly determine the cultural affiliation of human remains and objects to be repatriated.

Turning to the specific recommendations contained in the GAO report, we share the report's objective of maintaining an orderly, effective, and transparent program of repatriation. To this end, the Smithsonian will consider ways in which the role of Repatriation Review Committee could include some relationship with the repatriation program at the NMAI. Because, historically, the RRC has not been involved with the repatriation decisions rendered of the NMAI, the precise nature of the relationship will be the subject of further discussions with key stakeholders. The NMAI Board of Trustees brings the same scholarly credentials and cultural expertise to the task as the RRC. The NMAI Board of Trustees must by statute have a Native American majority; the Trustees collectively are knowledgeable of Native cultures and committed advocates of the preservation of Native culture. The Board plays the independent advocacy role that the Congress anticipated when it empowered the Board of Trustees with "sole authority" over the NMAI collections, subject to the general policies of the Smithsonian. Nonetheless, we recognize the benefit of working more closely with the Repatriation Review Committee and we are evaluating the most effective and efficient way to enable that.

We agree with the GAO that a system of periodic reporting to Congress on the progress of the Smithsonian's repatriation activities should be established. By virtue of the GAO's report, we recognize that Congress is indeed interested in the scope of repatriation on a national scale and the Institution will develop a reporting mechanism through which the Secretary of the Smithsonian can provide to Congress a complete picture of its robust and successful repatriation program.

The Smithsonian also agrees with the GAO that the process of appealing repatriation decisions by the two museums should be changed. We note, though, how rare it has been for repatriation decisions by the museums to be challenged. Indeed, in over twenty years, there have been only two cases in which a Smithsonian museum's decision was challenged. The collegial processes pursued by both museums and the roles played by the RRC and the NMAI Board of Trustees in the process have resulted, in the overwhelming majority of cases, in the acceptance of the museums' decisions by those who have requested repatriations.

In the interest of transparency and consistency, we are examining different procedures for appeals. We agree with the GAO that the decision maker on an appeal from a museum's decision should not have been involved in the museum's decision. We will consider different options and establish a new process that has these characteristics.

We agree with the GAO that the Smithsonian should adopt and publish policies for the handling of culturally unaffiliated items in the collections. We note that the Smithsonian's obligations with regard to such items are different from those established in NAGPRA. We believe, therefore, that our policies should not necessarily be the same as those established by the Interior

Department for NAGPRA institutions, and that such policies should be developed by the NMAI and NMNH in consultation with tribal governments. We will embark on such a consultation process promptly.

Thank you for the opportunity to testify, Mr. Chairman. I would be happy to answer any questions the Committee may have.

Index

J

K

L

M

N

O

P